RECEIVED 3 0

Quality Management for Software

K. Daily

MANCHESTER • OXFORD

British Library Cataloguing In Publication Data

Daily, Kevin.

Quality management for software.

I. Title

005.14

ISBN 1-85554-082-7

© Kevin Daily, 1992

All rights reserved. No part of this publication may be reproduced, stored in a retrieval system, or transmitted, in any form or by any means, without the prior permission of NCC Blackwell Limited.

First published in 1992 by:

NCC Blackwell Limited, 108 Cowley Road, Oxford OX4 1JF, England.

Editorial Office: The National Computing Centre Limited, Oxford House, Oxford Road, Manchester M1 7ED, England.

Typeset in 11pt Times by ScribeTech Ltd, Bradford, West Yorkshire; and printed by Hobbs the Printers of Southampton

ISBN 1-85554-082-7

To Elizabeth, Peter and Martin,
for their help and understanding.

Preface

Quality is sometimes likened to insurance. We don't miss it until we need it, by which time it is too late – and to do anything to solve the problem or repair the damage now requires considerable time and expense. Quality Management is how we ensure that work is done predictably and visibly and the products we intended to develop are produced when expected. We have to think ahead, make sure we know what has to be done, when and at what cost, and how we are going to do it. This is our 'insurance' against the consequences of producing products which are late, over budget and prone to error – that is, of poor quality.

If there is one saying which conveys the approach represented by Quality Management, it is, "Say what you're going to do, do it and show that you've done it". Quality Management is the set of practices, responsibilites, checks and records which achieve this throughout each project and work task.

Quality Management is implemented by means of a Quality System – the set of management and quality-related practices which are mandatory for projects and work tasks. Often, the Quality System will incorporate existing quality control and quality assurance practices, as well as introducing new ones.

In a Quality System, there is always evidence; we can examine project plans and records to find out what the project intended to do, what it has done and the extent of any deviations and problems which have occurred. Importantly, we now have a basis on which to predict whether the project can achieve its objectives and, if not, to decide what should be done.

Working on projects where a Quality System has been introduced is noticeably different than before – is particular it is more controlled and predictable. Every project and each work task is defined, planned, reviewed and approved. Progress and outcome is recorded and verified (eg by review) before the task can be deemed complete. Procedures regulate how the work is done and standards define the requirements for the types of product being produced.

Sometimes, Quality Management can appear somewhat time-consuming and even bureaucratic. If this is so, it is worth remembering the principle of 'structured common-sense' – if a procedure seems too detailed or a form too complicated, then is probably is. One of the skills of Quality Management is achieving the right balance between formality and practicality, and ensuring that the practices required make sense. Quality practices are only of value is they are feasible and contribute directly to achieving a sound product which is acceptable to the user.

The take-up of Quality Management for software and IT development has accelerated considerably. An important factor has been acceptance that the British standard for Quality Systems, BS 5750 (and its international equivalent ISO 9001) can be applied to software and IT work. It provides a 'formula' for the contents and structure of a Quality System and can be used as a basis for external certification of an organisation's Quality System. Because it is written in general terms, that standard needs interpretation and explanation for it to be used with confidence for software and IT work. One chapter is this book explains this standard and what it means in practical terms for project work.

This book is intended to explain what quality means for software and the contribution that Quality Management makes. This is the background to the chapters on software quality, which explain the practices of quality plans, review techniques, standards and procedures.

Introducing a Quality System within an organisation is a major task, requiring careful definition and planning. The chapter on this topic explains what is required and provides practical information to assist introduction.

The book includes a number of Appendicies which elaborate on topics covered in the chapters and are closely related to Quality Management. The development, production and maintenance of software needs to be thought of as a continuous life-cycle of stages, each with its own methods, techniques and quality requirements. One of the Appendicies provides examples of software life-cycles applicable to software work. Also, Configuration Management (the control of products and changes to them) is included since it is a topic closely affecting quality (and therefore is and integral part of any Quality System).

No two organisations will have exactly the same requirements for a Quality System, although the basic mechanisms and content will correspond. Sources of outside information are particularly useful in validating a Quality System and looking for gaps of inadequacies. The book therefore includes an Appendix which identifies and summarises available standards, guidance documents and other sources of information relevant to software and IT Quality Systems.

Introducing a Quality System should not be the end of the story. Like any system, it can always be better, and therefore capable of improvement. More efficient methods, better products and predictability for customers are important ways in which a Quality System will pay back the investment in time and money that is represents. Organisations find that a Quality System places them in a better position to embark on programmes of Quality Improvement and Total Quality, for example by adapting existing techniques such as Inspection and by introducing methods of defect analysis and problem solving. Techniques such as these, which can be readily introduced for software work, are also explained.

In summary, this book is intended to introduce the reader to the topics of Quality Management and to explain how it is applied to software and IT projects. Many of the basic principles are applicable to all types of project, but require explanation in software terms. Some practices, such as Inspection, can provide benefits even if introduced in isolation, outside a Quality System. Whether the reader is a quality professional, project manager, software developer or user, it is hoped that they will gain a better understanding of Quality Management from this book, and confidence that it can be applied to software.

Contents

	Page
1. Introduction	1
Achieving Software Quality	1
The Purchaser and Supplier	1
Obtaining Confidence	2
How the Product is Developed	3
Assessing Quality	3
Building Quality into the Product	3
The Quality System	4
Quality Management	4
The Importance of Quality	5
Planning Software Quality	6
How Does Quality Management Work?	6
Is Software Different?	7
External Assessment	8
Working Within a Quality System	8
Operating the Quality System	9
Quality Improvement	9
Purpose of this Book	10
2. Software and Quality	11
What is Software Quality?	11
Compliance to Requirement and Fitness for Purpose	11
Building in Quality	13
What Determines Product Quality?	14
Measuring Software Quality	16
Defining Software Quality	18
Software Product Usage	18
Product Characteristics	18
Characteristics, Criteria and Metrics	21
A Checklist Example	21
Using Quality Characteristics	23
The Quality System Approach to Quality	24

3. Standards for Quality Systems: BS 5750/ISO 9000 — 25

What is a Quality System? — 25
The BS 5750 Part 1 (ISO 9001, EN 259001) Standard — 27
   Quality Management Requirements — 28
   Technical (Project-related) Requirements — 32
   Support (Non Project Specific) Requirements — 36
Interpreting the Standard for Software: ISO 9000-3 — 40
   The Quality System Framework — 41
   Life Cycle Activities — 42
   Supporting Activities — 42
   Quality System Elements — 43
Summary — 44

4. Working Practices: Procedures, Standards and Codes of Practice — 45

Documented Working Practices — 45
How to Document Working Practice — 46
   Mandatory Documents — 46
   Advisory Documents — 47
Structure and Content of Procedures — 47
   Identification — 50
What Procedures and Standards are Needed? — 50
   Identification Standard — 50
   Procedure Standard — 51
   Implementation Procedure — 51
   Documentation Index — 52
   Documentation Set — 52
   Documentation Format — 52
Procedure Content — 53
   What a Procedure Should Tell Us — 54
   Standards Content — 54
   Codes of Practice — 55
   Work Instructions — 55
BS 5750/ISO 9001 Requirements — 55
A Documentation Set for Software Development — 56
   Quality System (General) — 57
   Quality System (Project-related) — 57
   Quality System (Project Specific) — 58
External Standards and Guidance — 59

5. Quality Control: Inspection, Review and Testing — 61

Introduction — 61
Inspection and test — 62
   How much Quality Control? — 62
   Verification Activities — 64

Reviews and Audits – What are they?	64
Levels of Control	65
Audits	65
Quality System Assessment and Legislation	67
What Project Reviews are Needed?	67
The Inspection Process	68
The Aim of Inspection	69
Conditions for Success and the Benefits	69
Personnel Roles	71
The Stages of Inspection	72
Design Reviews	77
Checklists	77
Prevention and Improvement	79
Prevention Techniques	79
Productivity and Defects	80
6. Documenting the Quality System: The Quality Manual and Quality Plans	**81**
Introduction	81
Organisation of the Quality System Documentation	82
The Quality Manual	83
What needs to be Documented?	83
A Checklist for Quality Manual Content	87
Quality Plans	88
The Contents of a project Quality Plan	88
Suggested Quality Plan Headings	89
Summary	97
Writing and Authorising the Project Quality Plan	97
7. Introducing a Quality System	**99**
Introduction	99
What is Involved?	99
The Introduction as a Project	100
The Stages of Introduction	100
The Need for Separate Stages	101
Stage 1: Preparation and Planning	102
Completing the Stage	103
Changing Methods and Practices	103
Stage 2: Introduction	103
Stage 3: Operation	104
Operation Stage Checklist	105
Stage 4: Assessment	106
Assessment Stage Checklist	106
Stage 5: Improvement	107
Improvement and Checklist	107

8. Quality Improvement and Total Quality   109

Introduction   109
Quality Improvement and Quality Systems   109
A Quality Improvement Programme   111
Managing Quality Improvement   112
Methods for Quality Improvement   112
    The 'Plan' Step   113
    The 'Do' Step   113
    The 'Check' Step   115
    The 'Action' Step   115
Problem Solving Techniques   115
    Brainstorming   115
    Why–Why Techniques   116
    How–How technique   117
    Force-Field Analysis   117
Quality Costs   118
A Typical Improvement Programme   120

Appendix 1 Configuration Management   123

Introduction   123
Configuration Management and Quality Standards   124
What is Configuration Management?   124
A Configuration Management System   125
    Version Control (Identification Control)   125
    Build Control   125
    Change Control   126
    Status Accounting and Reporting   126
Configuration Identification   128
Registration and Bonding: Item Status Bonding   128
A Documentation System   129
    Controls Required   130
Configuration Management Plans   131
Configuration Management Tools   131
Summary: the Benefits of a Configuration Management System   132

Appendix 2 Life Cycle Models   135

Introduction   135
Types of Life Cycle Model   136
    Sequential Models   136
    Cyclic Models   137
    Defining the Project Life Cycle   137
Life Cycle Models and Quality Systems   138

Some Life Cycle Models	139
The Waterfall Model	139
The 'V' Model	139
Incremental Models	140
Evolutionary Models	141
Life Cycle Models for Quality Planning	142

Appendix 3 Quality Records   147

Collecting Information	147
Designing Quality Forms	149
Mandatory and Guidance Content	150
Checklists	150
The Quality File	150
Sample Quality Forms	150
Quality Record	150
Inspection and Review Invitation	151
Review Checklist	152
Notes	153
Inspection and Review Report	153
General Points	154

Appendix 4 Quality Related Standards   157

Introduction	157
Relationship between External Software Standards and a Quality System	157
Quality Management System	158
AQAP 1	158
AQAP 2	158
AQAP 13	159
AQAP 14	159
Use of AQAp Standards	159
BD 5750 Part 1	159
BS 5750 Part 0 Section 0.1	160
BS 5750 Part 0 Section 0.2	160
ISO 9000-3	160
Other Quality System Standards	160
Quality Planning Standards	161
ANSI/IEEE 730	161
ANSI/IEEE 983	161
STARTS Purchasers' Handbook	161
Configuration Management	161
ANSI/IEEE 828	161
EEA Guide to Software Configuration Management	162

Documentation	162
BS 5515	162
ANSI/IEEE 830	162
JSP 188	162
Verification, Validation and Testing	163
BD 5887	163
ANSI/IEEE 829	163
IEEE 1012	163
Methods, Tools and Techniques	164
STARTS Guide	164
Other Guidance Material	164
STARTS Purchasers' Handbook	164
IT STARTS Developers' Guide	164
CCTA Infrastructure Library	165
The TickIT Guide	166
EEA Guide to Establishing a QA Function for Software	166
DEF STAN 00-16	166
Sources of Standards	167
Appendix 5 Quality Review and Audit	**169**
Types of Review	169
Technical Review	169
Management Review	169
Quality Review	169
Types of Audit	170
Vertical and Horizontal Audit	170
Audit Requirements of BS 5750/ISO 9001	170
The Role of the Auditor	171
Appendix 6 References and Further Reading	**173**
Index	**175**

1
Introduction

Achieving software quality

Everybody likes a good quality product − one which is easy to use, does the job that is required of it, is good value and can be obtained quickly and reliably. Quality is important for the supplier because it helps to sell the product and to generate further business. It is important for the purchaser because product quality can mean factors such as ease of use, reliability and efficiency, and meeting essential standards.

For the product supplier (or developer), quality cannot be relied on to come easily or cheaply, particularly when the product is as complex as software. Specific methods have to be used to identify and build in the quality required, including safeguards to check that it has been achieved. Additionally, the purchaser will need the confidence that the supplier can produce a good quality product; and so certain steps have to be taken which require the involvement of both purchaser and supplier.

The purchaser and supplier

Firstly, the purchaser must state his requirements: what product he wants, what he wants to use the product for and how he wants it to operate; also any standards (e.g. operational) which have to be met. The supplier then must ensure that he understands these requirements properly, so that he can identify the most appropriate methods he needs to both develop the product, and do it to the right quality. The supplier produces appropriate project plans, then monitors the progress and quality of the developing product against these plans.

In particular, the supplier detects and corrects faults and problems in the developing product (i.e. performs quality control), and periodically reviews whether the development methods and plans have been followed, and that the product has been checked against its requirements (quality assurance). All this is done within a framework of the supplier's organisational and project

2 Introduction

responsibilities, controls and practices, which are aimed at ensuring that he produces products which meet the purchasers' requirements (quality management).

When the product is complete, the supplier tests it before the purchaser evaluates it for acceptance. As part of this acceptance, the purchaser may require evidence that the project plans have been followed and that the product has been properly quality controlled and asssured during its development.

[margin note: NOT how we work]

Obtaining confidence

Specifying a product which has yet to be developed makes it difficult for either the purchaser or supplier to guarantee the outcome; there are many uncertainties, such as the extent to which the requirements are feasible, whether it can be developed within the required time and cost and, most importantly, will it work?

The sensible purchaser will want to take a number of precautions to reduce these uncertainties, so that he can have confidence in the outcome. In the first place, he will want to assess whether the developer is capable of providing the product he wants at the right level of quality, and that the supplier will be able to manage the development to produce an acceptable solution.

To do this, the purchaser will have to make sure he understands clearly the product that he wants, and how he will be able to recognise the right product when he has it, i.e. how the product can be shown to be acceptable. Also, he will decide how important are factors such as the correctness and completeness of the product (and any other specific quality requirements). He will take his requirements to a number of potential suppliers and get proposals from each of them. These proposals will identify what product they can supply, how they will develop it, what it will cost and how long it will take.

The purchaser will have to assess the proposals not just on cost and time to deliver, but on the approach the supplier takes to doing the work and how he manages the development of the product; he will look at the likely effectiveness of the supplier's approach to development since this provides evidence of capability and experience, and hence grounds for purchaser confidence. A further significant item of evidence is the practice of a supplier Quality System, particularly one that has been independently assessed by an external body such as the British Standards Institution (BSI). Such a Quality System represents the supplier's commitment to quality management practice, and will help the supplier and purchaser to work together in the way described above. The approach taken by the supplier to the work he does has to be properly defined, performed and controlled within this System, and with suitable responsibilities for these tasks.

How the product is developed

There is still a missing factor; there is no evidence to indicate whether the supplier can produce the specific product. This evidence comes from the way the supplier proposes to develop the product — the methods to be used and the controls to be applied. These methods and controls should be the ones suited to the type of work and, as far as possible, used regularly by the supplier for similar work. Even better, the supplier may offer the purchaser participation in development monitoring, for example by reviews of project progress, based on evidence such as compliance to project plans and the acceptability of completed work items.

Assessing quality

In most circumstances, it is unlikely that a purchaser will have the time or ability to be involved fully in the quality control and assurance of a development project — and in any case the supplier may be unwilling to allow such close surveillance. Instead, the purchaser can make use of the quality practices performed by the supplier. The supplier allows the development work to be monitored by internal personnel who are technically familiar with the type of work, but are independent of the development project. They are responsible not to the Project Manager but to a Quality Manager who is outside the normal project and line reporting structure. These 'QA' personnel are qualified to report on the effectiveness of the work and the methods used, to check that Quality Control has been done and if necessary can escalate problems to higher levels within the organisation. Their prime concern is the quality and acceptability of the final product.

Before the work starts, supplier QA reviews the project's quality plans, which also can be made available (in whole or in part) to the purchaser. The purchaser monitors achievement of the main milestones through the project by participation in periodic project reviews of progress against the plans. These reviews are, typically, at the end of each project stage, using quality control and assurance information from project work tasks as a basis of assessment.

Building quality into the product

All these measures provide confidence to the purchaser — the more the supplier is 'watched' by an independent QA function and by the purchaser and the greater the depth of 'watching', the more likely it is that problems will become apparent and be solved quickly, with the product required by the purchaser resulting. Quality is achieved by the combination of the methods employed by the supplier and by the internal and external monitoring of the supplier's

4 Introduction

work; confidence comes from seeing that the work has been done, by checking it against what was expected, and by establishing a defined level of collaboration between supplier and purchaser as the basis of this monitoring.

The extent and depth of monitoring (and the time and cost needed to do it) has to reflect the importance of the product to the purchaser, the extent of confidence that is needed, and how well the purchaser and supplier understand each other.

When the completed software product has been tested and delivered, from the point of view of quality the expected result can perhaps be summed up best as 'no surprises' – it may not be exactly the product the purchaser expected at the start of work, but as a result of his collaboration with the supplier and the resultant understanding of his problems, any changes will have been handled in a controlled way. The reasons and justification for any delays or changes will be understood and the decisions more easily taken than if they had been unknown to the purchaser or misunderstood by him (even if they were unavoidable).

The quality system

This approach to managing the quality-related aspects of a supplier's work can be formalised into a supplier Quality System which includes the elements of Quality Control (checking for errors and problems in the work), Quality Assurance (assessing independently the work done and the way it is done) and Quality Management (the organisational framework and associated responsiblities for quality). These quality practices can be applied to all types of industrial, commercial and professional work. The approach is perhaps summarised by the principle of:

> "Say what you're going to do, do it, and show that you've done it" – and if it's not right, correct it.

Quality management

Quality Management has been practised in many branches of industry (particularly defence and manufacturing) for some time, but it is comparatively recently that the software and IT sector has started to accept that quality-related practices like systematic Inspection and Review, compliance to Procedures and Standards, generation of Project Quality Plans and assessment of Quality Systems can be applied to itself – and can lead to real benefits of controllable projects, acceptable products for their customers and greater productivity and reduced costs for themselves. Similarly, purchasers of software products are realising the necessity of visibility of the development practice of their suppliers if they are going to be confident about receiving a product which is on time, at a reasonable cost and 'fit for purpose'.

The complete set of Quality Control, Assurance and Management practices needed for a supplier's operations is the Quality System (Figure 1.1) (sometimes called, perhaps more correctly, a Quality Management System or QMS). Significant numbers of software developers and suppliers are now considering the introduction of a Quality System, both for the internal benefits it brings and to respond to the increasing demand from purchasers for evidence of proper quality practices — equivalent to what purchasers have come to expect from other industrial and commercial sectors. Also, in the UK, the Department of Trade and Industry (DTI) has been encouraging British industry (including the software and IT sectors) to adopt practices such as Quality Systems and Total Quality Management (TQM) programmes to increase competitiveness.

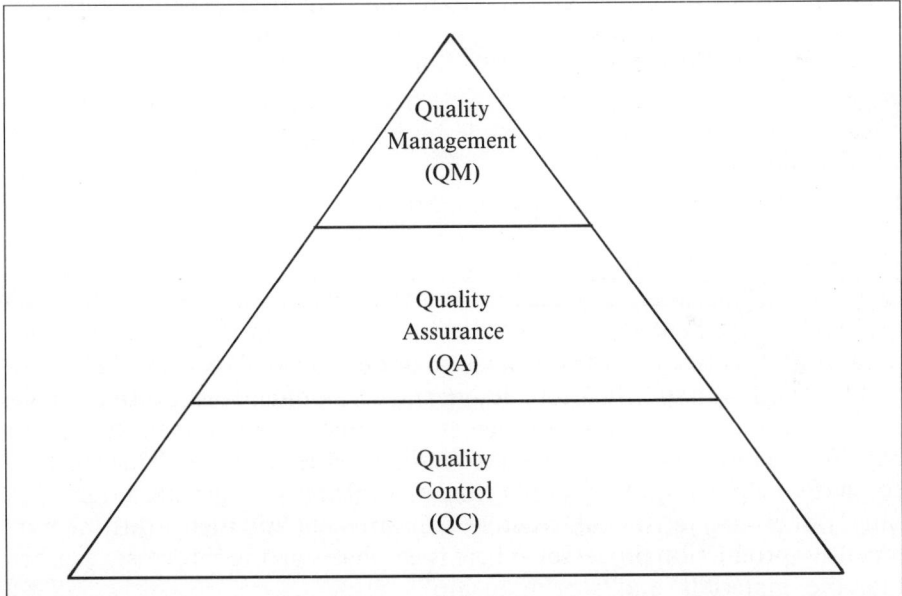

Figure 1.1 The levels of a Quality System

The importance of quality

The importance of software and IT systems within commercial organisations (where the typical supplier is the IT department and the customer is a user department), and in industry (where the supplier and purchaser are separate organisations), means that the software supplied must be a cost-effective, timely and effective solution to business and operational needs. A Quality System contributes to these aims by providing purchaser involvement and supplier visibility within the development process, and by ensuring that a recognised and proven set of quality-related practices is followed by suppliers.

6   *Introduction*

As a result, there is much interest from the software and IT community in topics such as Quality Systems, BS 5750 Certification, Quality Improvement initiatives, Total Quality Management programmes, etc. − and not just by software developers and suppliers, but by external purchasers and internal user departments. Both 'traditional' software purchasers such as the industrial and defence sectors (where the operational correctness and functionality of software is essential), and information-based organisations (where IT plays a vital operational and business role), are realising that quality of software is a very important management issue.

Get quality right, and not only is the software far more likely to meet the customer's needs first time, but commercial advantage is far more likely. Get it wrong, and increasing amounts of time and money are spent by both supplier and purchaser on coping with error-prone and inefficient systems, and consequently with resources underused and unproductive. It is still not unusual to hear of IT departments spending far more on maintenance than on new work − resulting in a long 'applications backlog' forcing users to look elsewhere or to wait longer for the systems they need. The resources to be released and the savings to be made by both supplier and purchaser are considerable.

Planning software quality

Quality Management as a way of achieving quality is important for software because of its nature and the way it has to be developed. Creation of software is almost entirely a specification, design and development task, with virtually no manufacturing or production element − replication may be no more than copying a set of files onto a disk for sending to the customer. This requires emphasis on 'pre-emptive' planning and control aimed at 'getting it right first time', rather than relying on 'reactive' measurement and then adjustment of repetitive production processes. There is emphasis on the 'processes', rather than the 'materials' and 'workmanship'.

This means that, before development starts, the methods and techniques which the developer intends to use are identified and evaluated, to ensure that the right ones have been selected for the type of work to be done − a Quality Plan defines how the product will be created, and shows how the right quality will be built in. This mandatory Plan includes the quality controls for every stage of work, and defines how it will be ensured that the methods and techniques are followed, and that the resulting products are acceptable.

How does quality management work?

The supplier's Quality System must be defined and managed against its own organisational objectives, assessed systematically and then corrected and improved where necessary. The system must be flexible so that it can be adapted for a new project or type of product. It must allow the purchaser to be involved at whatever level is appropriate to the product requirements (e.g. by review and monitoring of project quality plans). Also, a Quality System provides the supplier with a point of reference for existing practice, in particular quality-related activities such as Quality Control, Testing and Quality Assurance, which may have been introduced in a relatively uncontrolled way in the past.

It should be remembered that all organisations are both purchasers and suppliers – in its purchase of products or services for its own use, a supplier organisation acts as a purchaser, and can require the 'sub-contractor' to operate a supplier-role Quality System. In this way a 'chain' of suppliers and purchasers operate their own versions of supplier-role Quality System. Equally, everyone at some time acts as a supplier, even to another internal department or to the next work task of the project.

Is software different?

A common reason used to explain the difficulty of achieving good quality of software (and hence the feasibility of introducing a Quality System) is that software is different from other types of product and more difficult to handle – for example, software is intangible, needs its own approach to development and is inherently difficult to control. The software industry has experienced faster advance and changes in practice than any other which, it is argued, makes it hard to install 'conventional' practices like Quality Management. Certainly, software work is significantly 'one-off' in nature, in contrast to the production-line emphasis of manufacturing industry where many quality techniques were established. This means that many quality practices developed for industry need adaptation to software work, although still using the main principles of Quality Management.

Nevertheless, there are aspects of software work which are similar to the rest of industry. A project requires planning and proper resourcing to allow it to be managed properly and to deliver the required product on time and within cost. It needs defined and proven processes and practices, performed by personnel with the right skills and experience, and access to the right techniques and tools. The customer wishes to have confidence in the supplier by seeing evidence of his plans and methods before placing the contract, by monitoring the progress of work during the project, and by testing the completed product before accepting it. All of this should be possible for software, just as for any type of one-off project.

The interest shown by software and IT suppliers in working in this way is a sign of the increasing maturity of the software industry. A Quality System provides tangible evidence of a supplier's commitment to quality, i.e. the

8 Introduction

supplier must have recognised quality as being important to have gone to the trouble and expense of formulating, introducing and running a Quality System. The supplier must have sufficient confidence in his effectiveness to allow a purchaser or external body to assess his Quality System.

External assessment

The 'formula' for external assessment is the National, European and International Standards BS 5750, EN 29000 and ISO 9000 (they are identical in content). A formal Certification Body (such as the British Standards Institution) assesses an organisation's Quality System against this Standard and issues a Certificate if the assessment is successful. This is done widely in manufacturing industry, and is now starting to be taken up by software and IT systems suppliers (in 1990, approximately 30 such organisations, both large and small, had a 'Registered' Quality System). Following registration, operation of the Quality System is monitored by the Certification Body and registration can be withdrawn if the effectiveness of the Quality System is allowed to lapse. (NB: A similar assessment process of main contractors is performed by the Ministry of Defence against defence standards, most recently NATO standards AQAP1 and AQAP13. This is known as 'second party assessment', since it is performed and recognised only by the purchaser, whereas BS 5750 assessment is 'third party' as it is done independently and is intended for recognition by all purchasers.)

BS 5750 (and its equivalents) is a general specification for a supplier Quality System. The supplier defines the specific practices and methods within his Quality System by means of a 'Quality Manual' and associated working documents such as Procedures Manuals, so that a Quality System is defined in specific terms by its own organisation's business requirements and in general terms by the BS 5750 Standard.

Working within a quality system

A project performed within a BS 5750-type Quality System is recognisable by the quality-related practices that are followed and the way it is organised. The project team work to a set of Procedures and Standards which cover all the work that they do and the products arising. They review and inspect their products (including documentation), record the results and handle the problems which are found according to the Procedures and Standards.

The Project Manager's responsibilities now include the production of a Project Quality Plan to define the methods, practices, Standards and Procedures to be applied to the project ('how the work is done'). In most cases these will be proven ones which are used regularly for that type of work. If the project requires any of these practices to be adapted or replaced, the changes are defined and authorised in the Project Quality Plan. During the project, the Project Manager holds regular project reviews, not just to assess time and cost performance, but to assess compliance of the project to its Quality Plan. It is possible that a purchaser representative will participate in project-level reviews or other project reporting processes, and in some circumstances may perform his own assessment of particular aspects of the project (such as the completeness of test records).

Project work tasks will include some form of Inspection or Review of the products arising (equivalent to the testing of a software program before it is completed). In particular, all the main project documents will undergo this type of quality control.

A practice likely to be new to a supplier is Quality System Audit. A BS 5750 Quality System requires regular audit to provide evidence that it is being followed and that it is effective, both against the organisation's requirements and the BS 5750 Standard. This is done by (or on behalf of) the Quality Manager, whose line of responsibility is independent of project or line management and who reports directly to senior management. This means that any quality-related problems can be escalated for high-level decision if necessary. The Quality Manager is the 'custodian' of the Quality System, and must have sufficient authority to make it effective.

Operating the quality system

A supplier operating a Quality System need not employ teams of Quality staff; the quality-related practices should, as far as possible, be built into the project work and the management responsibilities and so be performed mostly by existing personnel, with the minimum of need for specific Quality personnel. Those that are needed can be seconded or 'borrowed' from other project work or operational areas as required. It is part of the 'culture' of a Quality System that it only requires specific quality staff where they are essential; it is the fulfilling of responsibilities and the achievement of day-to-day control which is important – an organisation can resource the Quality System in the ways that are most convenient to itself.

Quality improvement

An established Quality System need not stand still; a successful one leads naturally into improvement because the existing working practices are now defined and understood far better than before (including their weaknesses). A Quality System forms a 'platform' from which an organisation can advance into programmes and Quality Improvement or Total Quality Management –

the people and product oriented types of quality initiative, rather than the 'process' emphasis of the Quality System. Already, some software and IT organisations are starting to do this. The Quality System formalises the basic quality-related processes, which are added to or amended by the improvement programmes. This is the next stage of maturity of Quality Management after an effective Quality System has been established.

Purpose of this book

This book aims to explain the principles and practice of Quality Management as applied to software development and related work, using the BS 5750/ISO 9000 series standards as a 'formula'. It does not intend to replace the detailed information that can be found in existing Standards and Guides, and which in any case must be examined and understood before setting up a Quality System. Each chapter of this book includes references to where more detailed information can be found on the topics it has covered. This book explains the particular practices and features which a software-related Quality System will contain, and indicates what project practice will be like for those working within it.

While this book is framed around the typical software development project, similar principles and practices can apply to work such as enhancement of applications or selection of packages, provided that they are organised on a similar stage-by-stage project basis. Many of the practices covered, such as Inspection, can be used before a complete Quality System is established – one of the advantages of introducing a Quality System is that benefits from improved practice can be obtained before the full System is installed.

To summarise:

- a Quality System is a defined framework of quality-related practices for a supplier organisation;
- it includes Quality Control, Quality Assurance and Quality Management practices;
- it enables the supplier to manage the effectiveness and quality of a product or service and the way it is produced in order to meet the purchaser's requirements;
- it allows a supplier to provide the purchaser with evidence for confidence that his requirements will be met before and during a project;
- it allows a supplier to be independently assessed before work is done for the purchaser;
- a Quality System can be applied to software and IT systems work.

2
Software and quality

What is software quality?

We tend to view quality as something which is very desirable − products are sold on the basis of their 'quality', with the implication of excellence and hence desirability. This popular view of quality is judged by factors such as the way the product is designed, the materials that are used and its looks and appearance. The label of 'quality' may be accompanied by a higher price and different market position compared to other products of the same type.

We have to be careful in translating this view of quality into the industrial and commercial world. While a purchaser of a software product is unlikely to object in itself to excellence, the time it may take to develop and the associated cost may be less acceptable. From a business point of view, the product has to be justified by the benefits and advantages it brings − in viewing quality as excellence, the 70-30 rule is likely to apply, in that 70% of the work is needed to build the last 30% of quality. Is the extra time and cost needed to achieve excellence justified by the extra operational and business benefits?

Compliance to requirements and fitness for purpose

For a product (such as software) which has to be commercially and operationally successful, quality has to be primarily the extent of its compliance to requirements and within this, its fitness for purpose. Quality is therefore demonstrated by the extent of the product's conformance to requirements and the standard of this conformance. No matter how fault-free, well written or easy to use, the product has to provide the practical benefits required by the purchaser.

This view of quality means that the purchaser has an important contribution to make − first he must identify the business and operational (or user) needs for the product, formulate the corresponding requirements, and then agree with the supplier or developer what product can be provided to meet these requirements at a reasonable time and cost. The supplier/developer

12 Software and quality

responsibility is then to provide a product which meets the agreed requirements and to an acceptable standard; the purchaser's responsibility is to verify that this has been achieved. From the point of view of quality, these requirements fall into two main categories:

Product Requirements

- the product-specific functional and operational requirements, intended to meet the purchaser's identified needs.

Standards

- standards which define the 'goodness' and effectiveness of the particular product (e.g. operational reliability, user response times);
- general standards applicable to the type of product or to its operational requirements (e.g. conformance to industry test requirements, compliance to industry operating procedures).

These categories of requirement correspond to viewing product quality as being the extent to which it:

- complies with its requirements
- is fit for its intended purpose (Figure 2.1).

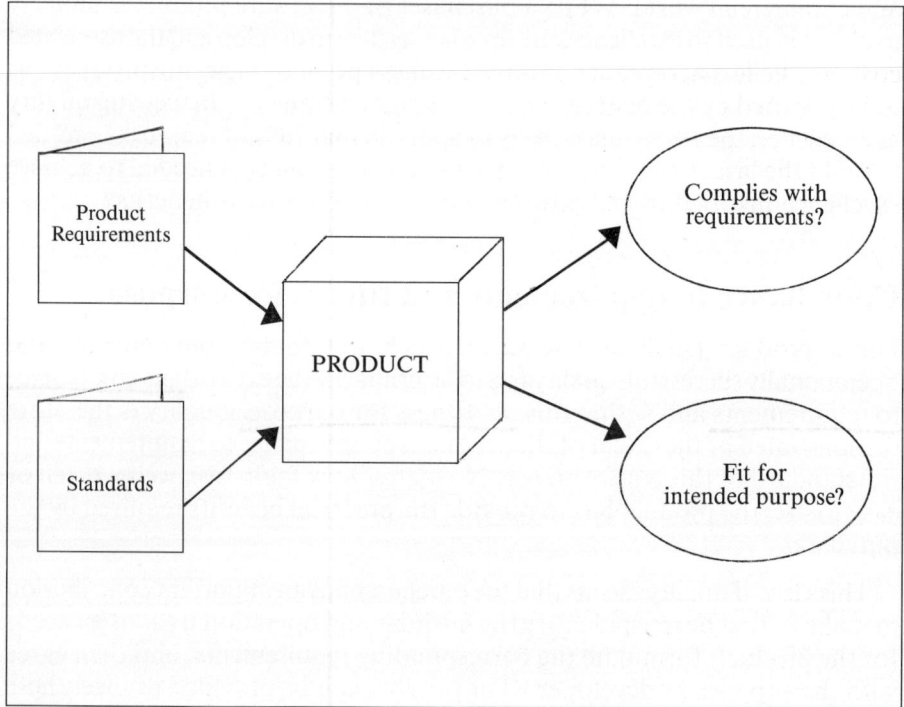

Figure 2.1 Defining and verifying product quality

Building in quality 13

Both forms of quality are measurable to the extent that, as long as the requirements are stated fully in a way that can be verified, the fact that they have been met can be demonstrated by the supplier and assessed by the purchaser.

Building in quality

The developer needs to ensure that the right content and quality of product is being created throughout the development process, which can be difficult for a complex product like software. However, waiting until the software is complete and ready for testing makes it very difficult and expensive to correct any problems (and makes it very unlikely that the product will be what the purchaser requires).

The developer addresses this problem by deciding what is the best set of methods to use before development starts and then ensuring that the methods and the products arising are regularly monitored at each stage of development. The methods should form a consistent life-cycle approach which can be relied on to convert the purchaser's requirements into an acceptable implemented product. While this approach is not fool-proof, it does increase significantly the likelihood that problems will be found earlier, and that experience will show which methods work well and which need improvement.

This approach to Software Engineering forms the basis of a Quality System, which requires that proper controls are in place throughout the development life-cycle to ensure that the most appropriate methods are used to produce the required product and to detect defects in either the products or the development practices, and also to correct these defects. These controls cover the technical, management, quality and support aspects of development work; everything which contributes to producing a compliant product which is fit for purpose.

The 'self-checking' features of a Quality System lead to gradual improvement of the effectivenss of development work (and the products), since experience of actual problems is fed back into the life-cycle methods. In effect, it is a 'belt and braces' approach, employing two different methods to achieve the same purpose; checking both the product as it is developed and the methods used to develop it, in order to ensure that the intended result is achieved, i.e. a product which satisfies the purchaser.

A Quality System helps to achieve a balance between time, cost, content and quality (Figure 2.2). For example, the Quality System controls should prevent a developer changing methods solely to save time, and therefore compromising the quality of the delivered product – at least, not without the change being properly reviewed, agreed and written into the Quality Plan for the project.

14 Software and quality

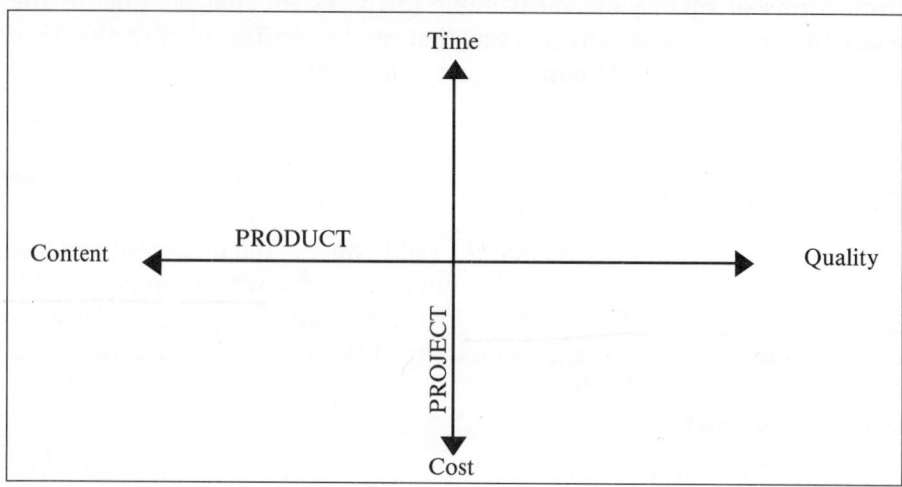

Figure 2.2 Balancing the project parameters

What determines product quality?

When viewing software as a commercial product, it is instructive to understand how product quality is viewed in manufacturing industry, since it is here that many quality practices have been established. The main difference for software is adapting these practices to a one-off development process, rather than a many-off manufacturing situation.

The British Standard definition of quality (from BS 4778) is:

"The totality of features and characteristics of a product that bear on its ability to satisfy a given need".

Like many definitions of this type, it requires further examination to understand it fully (Figure 2.3):

- The totality of features and characteristics: it is not one, but a range of product features which determine quality; also the term "characteristics" implies having to understand how the product features will work and how they will appear to the user.

- A given need: this indicates that the purpose of the product must be known and provides the basis for understanding the product's quality requirements.

This British Standard definition of quality starts from the customer producing a statement of market (or operational) needs for the product: why is it required, and what objectives must it achieve? Ultimately, quality of product determines the extent to which these needs are satisfied. These needs

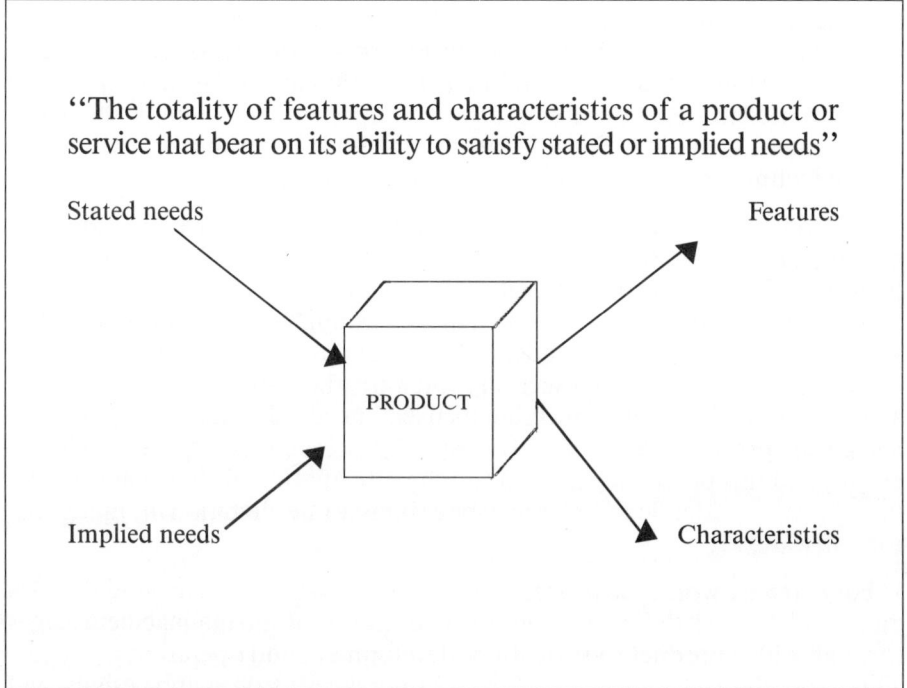

Figure 2.3. What is quality?

are then translated into a set of specifications and standards for the product. For software, this is typically a set of User Requirements which in turn is translated into Software Requirements by the developer. The developer will also need to consider the project requirements, and in particular the resources needed to create the software product, i.e. the technical, human and financial resources. These must be adequate, available and appropriate, or the product development process will suffer and it will not be possible to develop a product which meets its requirements and is fit for purpose at a sensible cost or timescale.

At this stage, trade-off of requirements against resources may be needed to ensure an acceptable balance of time, cost, content and quality. (These considerations should be part of the Contract Review and Project Initiation steps of a project.)

In this view of quality, manufacturing work requires three main elements: design, processes and materials. All three elements need to be adequate if the eventual product is to be satisfactory – a well designed product manufactured from poor materials or by inadequate processes will not be of good quality.

Design means identifying the components of the product (in software terms, the programs, data files, interfaces and other structures). The set of components must be complete, they must work together and must be capable of assembly into the complete product. Processes mean the techniques and methods used to identify and create these components, to assemble them into the product and to test it. For software this includes, for example, analysis and design techniques, programming, integration and testing.

Materials are the most difficult element to understand, since software does not consume raw material in the way a conventional manufacturing process does, and therefore its quality is not directly affected by poor material. But there is one feature of software which makes a similar contribution to quality – information. If wrong or inadequate information is supplied to an analyst, or incorrect data is input to executing software, the result will be the same – a poor product in terms of meeting its users' needs, despite otherwise good design and processes. Since all software will process data to a greater or lesser extent, and this processing is based on the information available at the time the software was developed, this may be a suitable interpretation of 'materials' for software.

For software work, the processes are selected and defined around the life-cycle model, which defines the succession of technical and management stages through which product specification, development and operation proceeds. This life-cycle model will generate the product specifications and designs, will obtain and provide the materials, components and information needed and define the methods to be used at each stage. Together, the stages form a consistent whole aimed at defining, producing and supporting a full operational system.

A key requirement for effective Quality Management of software is having a comprehensive life-cycle model for the product, whether it be a full product development with many stages including specification, design, coding and test and delivery, or a short enhancement or modification where a single stage of work will suffice. In either case, all the design, processes and materials required are attached to the relevant stages.

Measuring software quality

The test of a successful product must ultimately be the measures or indicators of quality. The conventional way of viewing quality is that there are two ways of measuring or expressing it:

- time independent
- time dependent.

A time independent measure indicates basic conformity to requirements, e.g. functionality, which will not vary with time. A time dependent measure may

Measuring software quality

vary with the occasion on which it is measured, and often will show a trend of variation, e.g. increasing failure rate, decreasing stability of performance.

Software shows interesting similarities — and dissimilarities — with this view of manufactured product quality. Some features (such as functionality) are likely to be more stable (time independent) for software than conventional products, because software does not wear out or degrade like a hardware product. Thus, an evaluation of software quality in terms of conformance to functional requirements made at system testing will remain valid (unless that part of the software is intentionally changed). Software functionality cannot change because the product degrades or wears out.

Some aspects of time-dependency in software arise because of changes in the way the software is used (for example increasing throughput of transactions) or because of incomplete testing (which fails to reveal hidden faults that are then left to appear when the software is used). In general, time-dependent aspects represent the apparent reliability of the product. While software does not 'wear out', many modern software products are so complex that it is impossible or uneconomic to test them completely before they are put into use — hence undiscovered problems come to light as the software is used more intensively (or sometimes in ways which were not originally intended!). This can give rise to an apparently increasing failure rate and thus decreasing reliability, particularly as usage increases. Conversely, this failure rate may then decrease once these problems are corrected and fewer hidden faults remain.

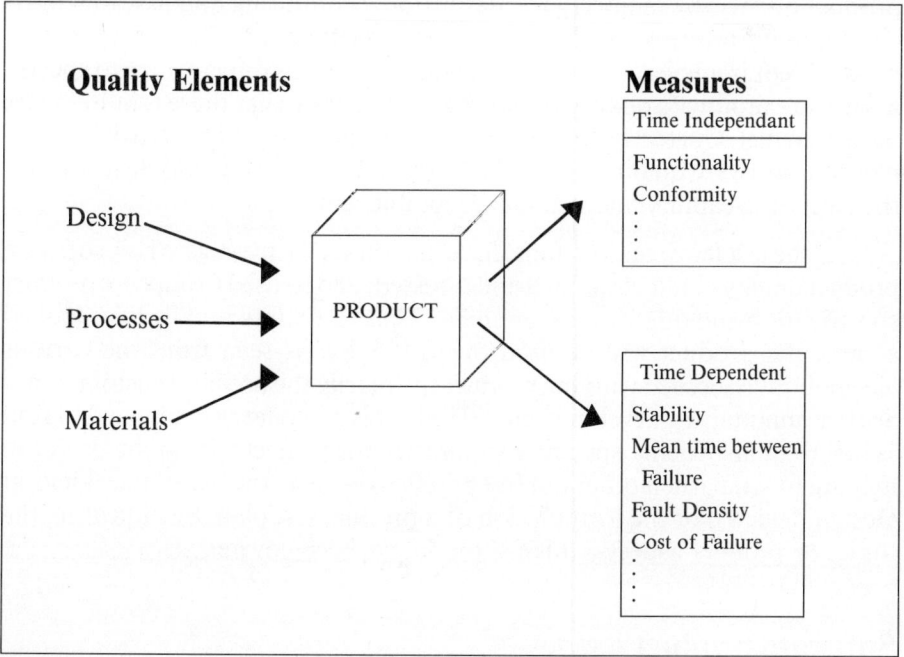

Figure 2.4 Measuring software quality

Typical time-dependent measures of product quality include (Figure 2.4):

- Stability (e.g. frequency of change)
- Mean Time Between Failure
- Fault Density
- Cost of Failure.

It is perhaps worth pointing out that System and Acceptance Testing practice for software tends to concentrate on Conformity (time-independent) measures, rather than on Reliability (time-dependent) measures.

The BS 5750 Standard for Quality Systems includes a requirement for statistical measures of product and process quality. This is being interpreted for software as a requirement to establish at least a basic programme of defect recording and trend analysis. Some software developers are starting to do this, as a first step to a future programme of software metrics (quantitative measures), for example, to help indicate areas of development practice which need improvement and to improve traceability between life-cycle phases.

Defining software quality

Quality Management principles emphasise the process elements of achieving product quality, by requiring the definition, monitoring and assessment of development processes in addition to the verification of conformance to product requirements – however, this does not tell us directly how to specify a software product's quality or how to demonstrate that these requirements have been met. Currently, this reflects lack of knowledge of how to define and measure software quality and an inability to verify this quality (e.g. what is the level of useability and is it an acceptable value?).

Over the last few years, attempts have been made to investigate how software product quality could be defined and assessed, and so used to improve product specification and quality measurement. These attempts usually have looked at how the product will be used operationally, as seen from the various viewpoints concerned with the product (primarily the user and customer, but also the maintainer, developer, etc.). While it is still relatively unusual to find software quality being specified so directly for projects, it can be useful in helping to strengthen other quality practices such as the use of checklists at Design Reviews, or the formulation of a product test plan, by indicating the topics or product aspects which should have been covered.

Software product usage

There are three types of usage to which any commercial or manufactured

product can be put:
- product operation (using it as it is);
- product revision (changing it for maintenance or modification purposes);
- product transition (re-using it for other requirements).

This approach allows us to identify a set of product quality requirements (or characteristics) which can be defined and measured as part of the product development. Alternatively, these can be used to assist review of product requirements, for example to identify significant omissions of information about the product.

Product characteristics

(i) Using the software as it is

The following set is suggested as a consistent and consecutive set of software product characteristics: i.e. they cover the various aspects of operating a stable software product and in general can be specified and assessed in the order stated. They can, of course, be adapted or extended as project circumstances require.

Useability   Can the software be used for its intended purpose?

Correctness   Does the software do what is required?

Reliability   Does the software continue to do what is required (i.e. continued correctness)?

Efficiency   Does the software do what is required with minimum resources, and within time and cost requirements?

Compatibility Does the software work (as relevant) with other required systems or software or to other external requirements?

Integrity   Is access to the operating software controlled and does this access only allow usage that is relevant?

A product needs to have **useability** (at least to the extent that it can show whether it meets the other requirements) before **correctness** is a concern. For instance, until a program can be loaded and run, the other characteristics cannot be demonstrated. **Reliability** (as defined here) is likely to be of relatively minor concern unless the software is undergoing modification. Nevertheless there need to be checks that, for example, the software produces repeatable results. Once the software is **useable, correct** and **reliable,** then **efficiency, compatibility** and **integity** can be considered in more detail.

20 Software and quality

(ii) Maintaining and modifying the system

Strictly speaking, software does not require maintenance in the usual sense, so the term is used to describe changes and corrections which are needed either because the software is faulty, it does not meet its requirements, or because the requirements themselves need to be modified (Figure 2.5). (Extensive rewrite is considered under the next heading.)

A relevant set of characteristics is:

Understandability   Is the function and structure of the software clear?

Modifiability   Can the software be changed?

Testability   Can the software be tested?

These three characteristics represent the principal steps of the maintenance process: first the software must be sufficiently documented for the required change to be identified and understood, then it must be capable of being changed, then finally it must be capable of being tested so the change to be checked. For instance, if no source code listings of a software product are supplied to the purchaser, then these characteristics will not be available — if the purchaser had wanted to be able to change the software, then he should have stated his requirements for maintenance in the Product Requirements.

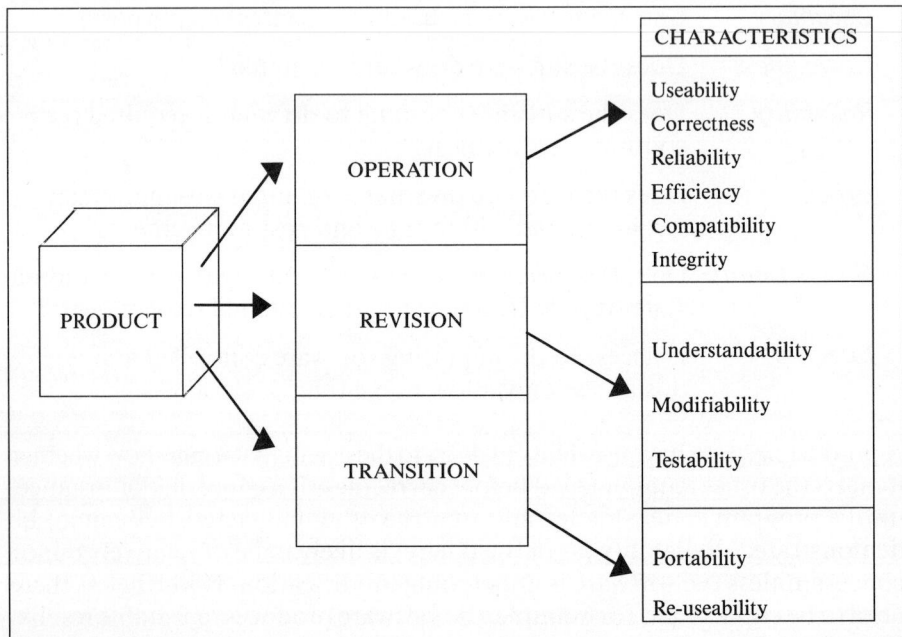

Figure 2.5 Defining software quality

(iii) Re-using the system

These characteristics apply to the situation where substantial alteration or change of use of the software is required — for instance if it is a package intended to meet different customers' needs for a particular type of application, or if its business requirement is to be substantially changed and so leading to a considerable re-write of the software. Another example is where the 'environment' of the application is to be changed; it is required to be ported to a different computer system or to run under a different Operating System.

Portability   Can the software function in a different environment (i.e. largely the same requirements)?

Re-useability   Can the software be used for different requirements?

The desirability (or even the need) for particular characteristics will depend on the viewpoint or role being adopted; for example, a user will in general require many of the first set of characteristics, but few if any of sets (ii) and (iii), since the latter are not usually relevant to a user role — indeed it should not be possible to allow a characteristic such as modifiability to be available to a user, except where specifically required. However, a developer may require re-useability so that the software can be adapted for other customer applications, even though an individual customer or user has no need for re-useability.

Characteristics, criteria and metrics

Some researchers have suggested establishing a hierarchy of more detailed definitions of product quality, starting with a set of management-oriented characteristics or factors (as above) and expanding each into more detailed, technically-oriented criteria which are meaningful to the development team and eventually quantitative metrics which are measurements of the products (and components) and the development processes (Figure 2.6). For example, Integrity would expand into factors such as Access Control, Security, Defensiveness (e.g. against invalid data), which in turn could be expressed where possible as numerical metrics (e.g. percentage of access requests rejected). In the interim, where it is not practical yet to perform quantitative measurement, checklist questions can be substituted to be used for appropriate levels of product and document review.

A checklist example

The following example illustrates how a checklist for reviewing a Requirements Specification can be generated for some of the characteristics defined above; the individual questions here are product-oriented to reflect a developer's need

22 Software and quality

to review the document to find where it may be inadequate to use as a basis for development.

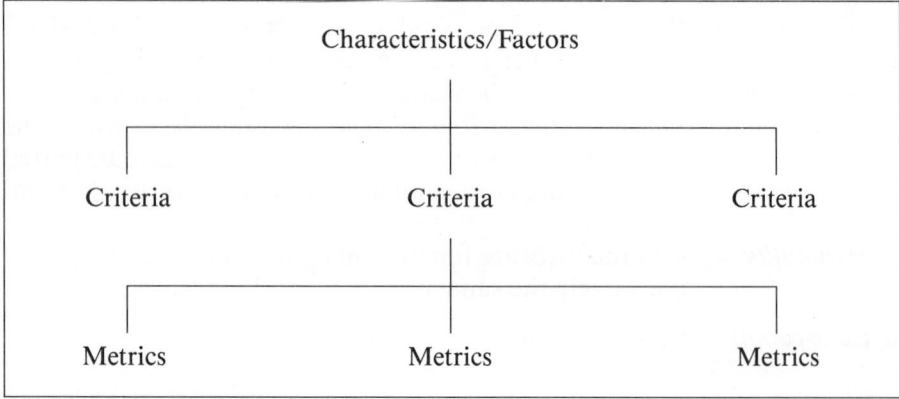

Figure 2.6 Characteristics, criteria and metrics

Useability
- Does the Specification define specific user operating procedures which must be provided?
- Are requirements for operability such as typical or maximum response times stated?
- Are user screen formats and layouts defined?
- Are training targets such as typical operator familiarisation time stated?

Reliability
- Is there any stated target for mean time between software failures?
- Is there any requirement for error tolerance?
- Will specific measures be needed to protect data from corruption?

Portability
- Is the software required to operate on more than one hardware/operating system environment?
- Will re-compilation of the software be required to port it to another environment?

This approach to software quality could apply, of course, to any product, including hardware. It is particularly relevant to improving the specification (and associated testing) of software to ensure that specifications include more than just functional and operational aspects. One difficulty in doing this is

Using quality characteristics

the time it takes to produce detailed specifications of a particular characteristic (e.g. efficiency), and in terms that can be tested.

Further information

One of the best sources of further detailed information on this topic is Tom Gilb (see References in the Appendicies), who has shown how these characteristics (or "attributes") can be defined in detailed and testable form. A characteristic is broken down into individual testable criteria by defining:

- the measurement unit or scale (e.g. time to reload software following a system crash);
- measurement range (e.g. worst acceptable, expected level and best achievable).

Tests of the relevant features of the software against each criteria can be defined, and the outcome demonstrated. (This can also form a useful starting point for Quality Improvement initiatives, by indicating the current situation, implementing a change and then repeating the test to demonstrate whether a targeted improvement such as 50% reduction in maximum loading time has been achieved.)

Using quality characteristics

In practice, it is likely that this type of approach will be taken up for quality characteristics which are important to achieve (Figure 2.7) particularly if they are business or operationally critical to the product. Their detailed definitions can than be written into the Product Requirements and corresponding Test Requirements, and used as a basis for checklists applied to Inspections and Reviews during development, and specific tests during acceptance.

Importance	Test Criteria	Non-compliances
Essential/Critical	Demonstrated comprehensively	None
Highly desirable	Must be demonstrated	Very few
Desirable	Demonstrate adequately	Some allowable
Optional	Can be demonstrated	Noted
Not required	Show abscence	None

Figure 2.7 Using Quality Characteristics

24   *Software and quality*

A useful way of focusing on the important quality requirements is by defining the comparative importance (criticality) of the various characteristics and criteria, for example:

- essential (critical)
- highly desirable
- desirable
- optional
- not required.

This assessment can be used to formulate corresponding testing criteria:

- must be demonstrated comprehensively (product unacceptable otherwise);
- must be demonstrated (only very few/very minor non-compliances acceptable);
- should be demonstrated to an adequate extent (some non-compliances acceptable);
- can be demonstrated to show presence (achievement not necessary for delivery);
- should be tested to show absence.

These criteria represent a weighting of importance of the various quality requirements and therefore allow attention to be concentrated on the most important requirements for that particular product.

The quality system approach to quality

A Quality System represents a different, but complementary, approach to achieving product quality. It ensures that the processes used to develop a product are consistent with the product's requirements. There is no reason why a selection of quality characteristics cannot be included in these requirements. The Quality System then requires that there is a corresponding set of quality processes (such as Design Review, Inspection, Testing and Document Control) to evaluate the achievement of the quality characteristics.

3
Standards for quality systems: BS 5750/ISO 9000

What is a quality system?

Any business or operation needs to perform a certain mimimum set of activities to do its work efficiently and effectively. It needs to know what types of product or service it is providing, what methods, techniques and working practices it uses to create these products and services and what kinds of checks are needed to ensure that they are acceptable to the purchaser. This framework of management, technical, and quality activities is the Quality System; it is there to ensure that the right controls are provided so that a product or service acceptable to the purchaser is produced consistently and predictably.

It can be suprising how often this framework is missing or only partially established in an organisation, including those involved in the development of software or IT products. While software is often complex and difficult to test in a realistic way, many quality problems are caused by factors such as poor planning and control, insufficient documentation and inadequate testing. It is these aspects of development which will become much more properly organised and effective within a Quality System (Figure 3.1).

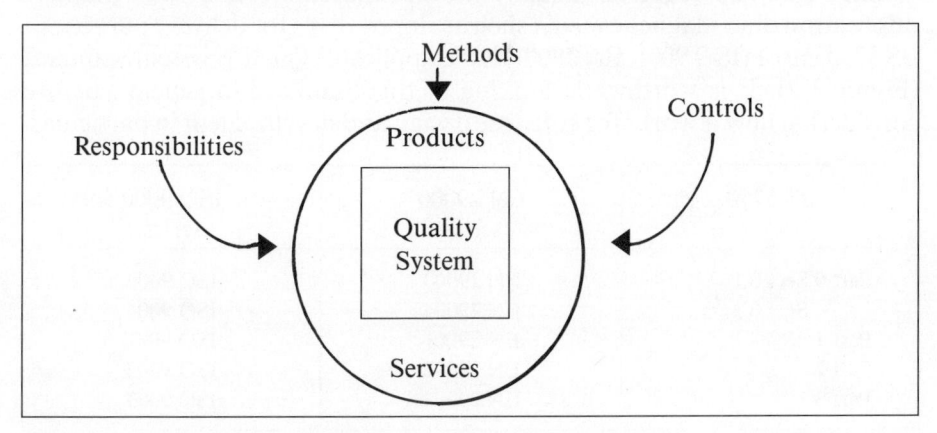

Figure 3.1 The Quality System

The Quality System is a concept which originated in industry (particularly defence and manufacturing) and has been adopted there with much success. In 1979, the British Standard BS 5750 was published, which provides a Specification for the minimum content of an organisation's Quality System. It was updated and republished in its current form in 1987, alongside the International Standard ISO 9000 – the two are identical in content. Also, there is a corresponding European Standard EN 29000.

While it is common for a company to introduce a Quality System which covers all its commercial activities, the System can be restricted to specific parts of an organisation or even to particular activities – as long as the scope of the Quality System is clearly defined. In fact, it is not unusual for software or IT activities to be brought into a company's Quality System after its production or operational areas, particularly where they support these activities rather than being itself the main commercial activity.

BS 5750 is in fact a series of documents (Parts 0 to 3), corresponding to the International Standards ISO 9000 to ISO 9004 and European Standards EN 29000 to EN 29004. Part 0 contains two Sections, 0.1 and 0.2. BS 5750 Part 0 Section 0.1 (i.e. ISO 9000, EN29000) is an introductory document which explains the subsequent Standards documents BS 5750 Parts 1 to 3 (ISO 9001 to ISO 9003, EN 29001 to EN 29003). These Parts define the Quality Systems applicable to different types of manufacturing or commercial situation – where work is primarily Production and Installation (Part 2) or primarily Final Inspection and Test (Part 3). For simplicity, in most instances this book will refer to these sets of Standards as BS 5750/ISO 9001, although it is actually BS 5750 Part 1 (and hence ISO 9001) which applies to the design and development process, and hence to software development. BS 5750 Part 0, Section 0.2 is a "Guide to quality management and quality system elements", which is identical to the documents EN29004 and ISO 9004.

Since software requires virtually no manufacture (other than perhaps duplication onto magnetic media such as floppy disks for delivery purposes), BS 5750 Part 1 (ISO 9001, EN 29001) is the applicable Quality System Standard (Figure 3.2). It is worthwhile looking at this Standard in general, before considering how it works for software design and development in particular.

BS 5750	EN 29000 series	ISO 9000 series
Part 0 Sect 0.1	EN 29000	ISO 9000
Sect 0.2	EN 29004	ISO 9004
Part 1	EN 29001	ISO 9001
Part 2	EN 29002	ISO 9002
Part 3	EN 29003	ISO 9003

Figure 3.2 BS 5750 / EN 29000 / ISO 9000 Standards

Note that the following description of the BS 5750/ISO 9001 Standard for Quality Systems is intended to introduce and explain it; the full Standard (available from BSI) must be examined for a complete understanding of its content.

The BS 5750 Part 1 (ISO 9001, EN 29001) Standard

The main part of the Standard comprises twenty paragraphs (with many broken down into more detailed sub-paragraphs), each of which describe a particular requirement (element) of the Quality System. These requirements are summarised in software terms below.

In understanding the Standard, it has to be remembered that it applies to the 'supplier'; this is the organisation which is operating the Quality System. The products and services are supplied to the 'purchaser', usually an external, contractual, customer but it can be taken to mean an internal customer or user department within the same organisation. Services or products purchased by the supplier come from 'sub-contractors', again either external to the organisation or from another internal department.

Quality Management	Technical	Support
Management responsibilities	Contract review	Product identification and traceability
Quality policy and organisation	Design control	Document control
The Quality System	Process control	Inspection and test status
Management review	Inspection and testing	Purchasing
Internal quality audits	Inspection, measuring and test equipment	Purchaser-supplied product
Corrective action	Control of non-conforming product	Statistical techniques
	Handling, storage, packaging and delivery	Quality records
	Servicing	Training

Figure 3.3 BS 5750 Part 1/ISO 9001 requirements

The requirements of BS 5750/ISO 9001 cover all aspects of quality-related work required in a commercial or professional situation: technical, quality, management and support practices (Figure 3.3). It is a general standard in that it is not specific to any particular industry or process. The supplier organisation defines a specific Quality System to cover its own set of products and services and working practices; BS 5750/ISO 9001 then acts as a statement of requirements for the organisation's more detailed Quality System. It does not specify the products, methods or processes to be used, except in general terms;

the supplier has to identify and document these as part of its own Quality System. To assist understanding, these requirements are classified below to indicate whether they are related primarily to quality management, technical or support practice, although this is not done by the Standard itself. (Note that some of these requirements may include or cover more than one type of practice.)

Quality management requirements

These are requirements which relate mainly to the setting up and operation of the Quality System.

Management responsibilities: quality policy and organisation

A fundamental requirement of a Quality System is that management objectives, structure and responsibility for the quality of products and services is known and defined − running from the most senior levels down to the operational and project levels. The Standard requires that management produces ("defines and documents") statements of Quality Policy and Quality Objectives and that it records its commitment to policy. In practice this can be done by a short statements included in the company's Quality Manual, which is one of the the Quality System documents described below.

An organisation's structure must be defined to cover everyone's duties relating to quality − in practice, because it must be clear how these quality responsibilities relate to other management responsibilities, a complete management structure is usually included. The Standard requires that the "duties, responsibilities and authority" are defined for all staff who "manage, verify, or perform work affecting quality". In practice, the roles, responsibilities and reporting structure are stated, but not specific personnel names, so that this information only needs to change if the organisational structure changes.

Organisations which already have a Quality Assurance function should find it easy to fit this into the Quality System − provided that it meets one of the prime requirements, that it has independent reporting lines to a "senior management representative", usually a senior manager or director who has been assigned the responsibility for quality. However, the standard does not specifically require a separate QA function, just that there is a "management representative" who is the focus of all quality matters, and whose responsibilities and authority are defined within the organisational structure. In practice, most organisations appoint a Quality Manager to perform this role − sometimes in a large company, there may be several such managers covering different parts or types of operation, while in a small organisation, the Quality Manager may have other responsibilities as well (e.g. Systems Manager). In the latter case, care must be taken to demonstrate that there is no conflict of responsibility (e.g. by requiring delegation of authority when necessary).

Quality management requirements

A Quality System does not limit responsibility for quality to the Quality Manager. The Standard stresses that everyone contributes to quality by their work role for the product or service (Figure 3.4). There will be procedures which state personnel responsibilities for the work they perform.

While the standard does not explicitly require 'QA' staff, it requires that staff involved in verification of products and processes (or of the Quality System itself) are properly skilled and trained for the purpose. It will have to be clear who is responsible for such verification work and what technical, process and 'QA' knowledge is needed – and whether these staff are full-time QA or doing this on an occasional basis.

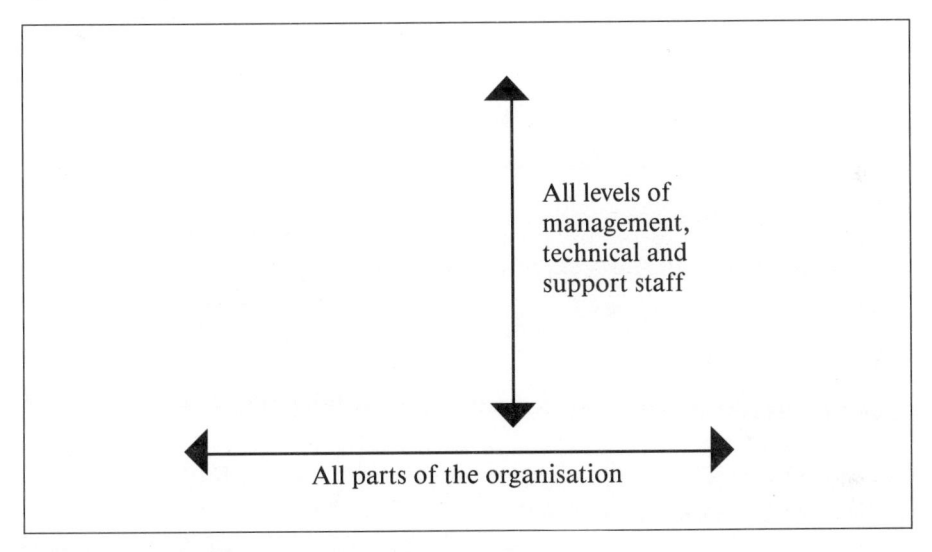

```
                    ↑
                    │  All levels of
                    │  management,
                    │  technical and
                    │  support staff
                    ↓
    ←───────────────────────────────→
         All parts of the organisation
```

Figure 3.4 The responsibility for quality

One consequence of this requirement is that if the organisational structure changes as a result of reorganisation (including mergers or takeovers), this part of the Quality System may need to be changed to ensure that the correct reporting responsibilities for quality are retained.

The quality system

The Standard requires that the complete Quality System is defined and documented. An important reason is to demonstrate precisely how the organisation's Quality Policy is achieved in practice. This shows that there is a sufficient set of activities and procedures which contribute to the quality of its products and services and that they are applied in practice. It is useful to indicate at this point how product quality is viewed (e.g. timeliness of delivery, completeness of the product), reflecting the supplier's understanding of the market needs for its products.

30 Standards for quality systems: BS 5750/ISO 9000

It is particularly important to identify the procedures and working practices which apply to the work being done (such as the preparation of Quality Plans) and how they are monitored and evaluated (e.g. review and inspection techniques). The basic rule is that any feature of work which is potentially a risk to the quality (effectiveness) of the processes and products should have some procedure or control method defined for it — and all information about the work processes and products should be held as some form of quality record. These aspects are described more fully below. (When a Quality System is assessed against BS 5750/ISO 9001, this requirement can be used to indicate whether the System is complete as well as consistent with the Standard.)

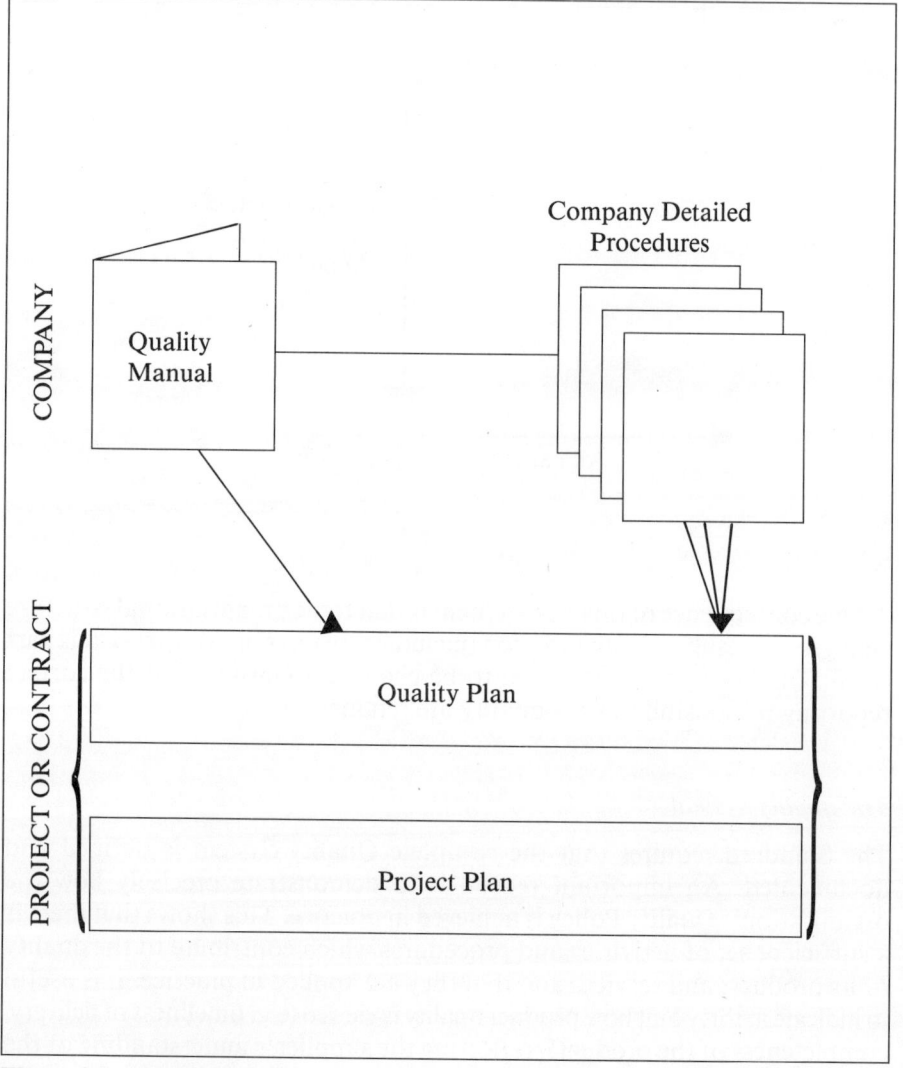

Figure 3.5 Quality system

While the Standard does not lay down a particular structure of documentation, the most common way is to create a Quality Manual for the company-level information and a separate set (or sets) of Procedure Manuals for the day-to-day working practice described in Quality Plans (Figure 3.5). The Quality Manual is usually a fairly slim document containing the Quality Policy, definition of organisational structure and other high level information, together with references to the other documentation within the System. It needs to be stable (i.e. infrequent amendment) and therefore should include a minimum reasonable level of detail. Also, importantly, it is a document which the supplier should feel free to show to external customers without risk to commercial confidence, and so it will not contain proprietary or detailed information such as might be found in the Procedure Manuals.

Procedures can be grouped and distributed to the appropriate operational areas or project teams. They can be as restricted in distribution as required. They describe the processes that are performed in developing the products and services, as well as the associated responsibilities and actions that contribute to quality. (In practice, this usually means that all technical, management, quality and support processes relevant to the work content are described in the set of Procedures, since ultimately they all contribute to product quality.)

It is important that the procedures are neither too detailed (which will make them difficult to adhere to and disliked by staff) nor too sketchy, in which case they will not be effective. They must be written in such a way as to be capable of verification. Procedures can be held partly or wholly on the computer system if preferred, as long as their availability and access to staff is controlled in an equivalent way to documentation distribution controls (e.g. by password).

Management review

A very important requirement of a BS 5750 Quality System is a periodic management review of its overall effectiveness (and of compliance to the Standard). Typically, this is done every six or twelve months by the Quality Manager as a formal Review (based on information from a programme of more specific internal Quality System Audits over this period). The results of this Review must be recorded and acted upon; for example, specific corrective action must be taken if working procedures are found to be inappropriate or are not being followed.

Experience shows that Management Review of the overall quality of an organisation's operations is unlikely to take place until a Quality System is installed, yet the benefits of this form of Review are likely to be considerable. The Quality Manager will be able to identify weaknesses in practice, either generally or in specific projects or types of work (e.g. system testing), and ensure action is taken to correct the problem at whatever levels are appropriate (project, line management, company, etc.).

32 Standards for quality systems: BS 5750/ISO 9000

Internal quality audits

As part of the management responsibilities for quality, a comprehensive series of internal Quality Audits must be performed (by, or on behalf of, the Quality Manager). The objective is to ensure that the Quality System is being complied with and that it is effective, and as a result, is identifying areas where alteration or improvement is needed. It is typical for the Quality Manager to plan a series of audits over the year, which together cover all aspects of the Quality System, and allow time for repeat or more detailed investigation where any aspects of work practice are found to be deficient.

Another important reason for performing internal Quality Audits is that any external assessment of the System against the BS 5750/ISO 9001 Standard will require evidence of regular internal audit – without this evidence, external Certification of the Quality System cannot be achieved.

Corrective action

Inspection and Test of items, and proper handling and identification of non-conformance is of limited value if the problems and faults are not corrected. The Standard requires specific procedures for corrective action, covering both internal and external products and services; this is not just to correct the problem, but to prevent the problem happening again – which implies analysing why it occurred and what change or tightening of practice may be necessary.

The Standard requires that specific corrective action takes place. This can be done following Inspection or Test work, or by holding regular corrective action meetings to analyse quality records (e.g. non-conforming product). Potential problems should also be considered where they may affect the products or processes.

Technical (project-related) requirements

These are requirements which relate primarily to project specific work.

Contract review

Contract (and project) work must be reviewed before it is committed to, e.g. are the requirements known and understood, what contractual (or legal) obligations are there, are the right skills and resources available to do the work? This requirement can also be applied to internal 'contracts', for example, by means of an internal Project Initiation process.

One consequence of this requirement is that a contract or project should not be entered into if there is insufficient resource or, for example, there are

Technical (project-related) requirements 33

known significant problems with the requirements, i.e. where there is an obvious risk to the quality (acceptability) of the final product or to the supplier's ability to do the work within the required time or cost.

Design control

In the Standard, the term "Design" covers the process of developing the product, rather than the more specific design process as applied to software. Thus, in software terms, Design Control applies throughout the development process. The Quality System must include stages of:

- design and development planning
- design input
- design output
- design verification
- design changes.

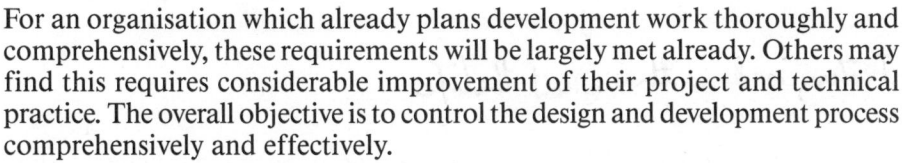

For an organisation which already plans development work thoroughly and comprehensively, these requirements will be largely met already. Others may find this requires considerable improvement of their project and technical practice. The overall objective is to control the design and development process comprehensively and effectively.

Examples of the requirements within Design Control include:
- technical responsibilities such as for the design integrity and its verification;
- control of interfaces and liaison with other organisational and technical groups;
- preparation and maintenance of documentation;
- regulatory and standards requirements;
- establishment and maintenance of design review procedures.

Process control

On first sight, this requirement is straightforward — "production shall be identified, planned and carried out in controlled conditions", but for software work this can require significant tightening of practice. A typical solution is to produce detailed project plans (or equivalent) which define the stages of work, the tasks to be done, the methods, techniques and tools to be used and state (or reference) the required procedures — in other words, the life-cycle model for the project. Procedures and work task definitions may need to be elaborated as detailed 'work instructions', either for clarification or where a variation or restriction on the normal procedure is necessary. The key requirement is that the project can demonstrate what work is being done, how it is being done, and how the outcome will be verified (and if not satisfactory, that the problem will be found and handled properly).

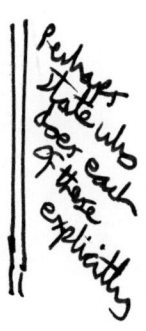

34 Standards for quality systems: BS 5750/ISO 9000

Some of the more detailed requirements include:
- definition of how the work is done (i.e. methods, techniques), particular 'equipment' (e.g. tools) and the working 'environment' (e.g. particular development facilities);
- on what basis the results of the work can be evaluated by inspection or verification (e.g. how can the design be checked).

This part of the Standard requires monitoring procedures for "special processes where results cannot be fully verified by subsequent inspection". This means that, where a process cannot be fully verified or tested, there must be some form of monitoring to assess whether the process is working properly or at least capable of detecting problems.

This requirement also calls for installation processes to be planned and carried out, which for software may range from simply including an adequate Install function (or at least comparable instructions), to producing an Installation Plan for a major application for a mainframe.

Inspection and testing

[handwritten: Testing is done throughout the life]

At first sight, comparatively little of the content of the Standard is concerned directly with product Inspection and Testing, reflecting its emphasis on preventative and preparatory practices as much as on fault finding. However, its requirements for Inspection and Testing, when applied to software, are likely to increase this type of practice in the earlier stages of development, when often comparatively little software verification has been done.

The Standard calls for three stages of Inspection and Test: Receiving; In-process; Final, and the creation of records of their performance and the results.

Receiving Inspection and Test is intended to prevent faulty components being incorporated or developed further; for instance, a faulty design being used for programming work, or a defective program being incorporated into an application. This should be done from the viewpoint of the receiver of the item (e.g. the programmer should be satisfied that the design about to be coded has been inspected).

In-process Inspection and Test is done from the viewpoint of the developer/creator of the item, to demonstrate that the item meets its requirements. The Standard requires that there are documented procedures for this. [handwritten: Prog Mod system]

Final Inspection and Test has two intentions: it demonstrates that the complete product or service meets its requirements, and ensures that the previous checks at earlier stages have been done and are satisfactory. Hence, without proper Receiving and In-process checking, Final Inspection cannot be completed. [handwritten: Jacks end testing]

All of these checks have to be recorded as a set of Inspection and Test Records, to provide evidence that the product (and its components) have been checked against their requirements.

For projects, the creation and performance of test plans contributes to this requirement, provided that they contain the information described above.

Inspection, measuring and test equipment

On first sight, this paragraph of the Standard may seem to have little relevance to software work. In a manufacturing environment, it ensures that equipment used to make test measurements is itself properly adjusted and calibrated (where possible to external standards), and that its limits of accuracy are known. There are some parallels in software, for instance where a test program or system is used to test the developed software (e.g. by simulating operating conditions or external processing requirements such as communication protocols). This paragraph can be interpreted to require such test programs themselves to be verified – or at least for their full specification to be known and assessed for suitability for the test requirement.

Control of non-conforming product

It is important to identify items which have failed Inspection or do not conform to their specification. A suitable procedure will be needed to meet this requirement and, wherever possible, to identify these items to prevent them being used further. For example, on a development system, such software items should be held in files or catalogues which are not directly accessible to programmers, with the items being clearly documented as non-conforming. For documents, these should be held separately, e.g. in a different file, from accepted ones.

There must be someone responsible for reviewing non-conforming items and deciding what action to take, so that they are reworked, corrected or whatever is appropriate (e.g. revision of the item's requirements). (These items should not continue to be non-conforming for any longer than necessary.)

Handling, storage, packaging and delivery

This is another requirement which at first sight might seem to have little relevance to software; but it is intended to prevent deterioration, misuse or damage of products, which can happen to software just as with any product. Procedures are needed to cover these requirements from the time of receipt of an item, through the development process to storage, transit and delivery. Included is the need for proper packing and marking. Examples for software include:

36   *Standards for quality systems: BS 5750/ISO 9000*

- handling and storage of floppy disks (and other magnetic media);
- file and catalogue structure and access for software held on computer systems (e.g. to prevent unauthorised access);
- storage and packing of customer documentation;
- delivery and receipt of software and documentation.

It is important to inform the customer of any special requirements for software (e.g. storage of magnetic media, acknowledgement of delivery) which form part of the supplier's procedures (i.e. primarily are part of the development process) and ensure that the customer follows them.

Servicing

This requirement is applicable "where specified in the contract", to make it clear that servicing (i.e. support) of a delivered product is not mandatory. Where it is done, there must be procedures for both carrying out the servicing or support and checking that it meets requirements (which implies that these requirements are stated as part of a contract). In an internal situation, the contract might be replaced by a Service Level Agreement which defines the level and content of support.

Support (non project specific) requirements

These are requirements which are mostly not specific to projects (although they apply to all projects), and therefore can be met by general procedures and practices.

Product identification and traceability

This requirement is largely self-evident, in that the product (and, by implication, its components) has to be identifiable through all its development and design stages, from specification through to delivery. One reason is to allow defects in the delivered product or service to be traced back to their origin, e.g. a fault in the design of a component. Where multiple deliveries are made (e.g. at different times and/or to different customers), these 'batches' must be identifiable.

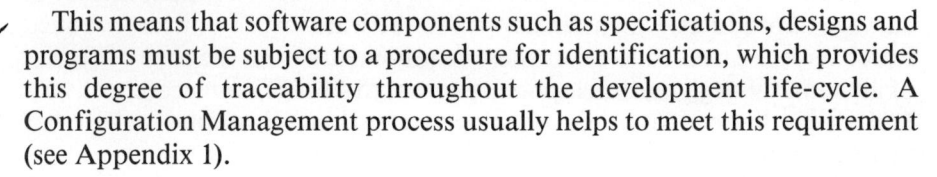

This means that software components such as specifications, designs and programs must be subject to a procedure for identification, which provides this degree of traceability throughout the development life-cycle. A Configuration Management process usually helps to meet this requirement (see Appendix 1).

Support requirements

Document control

Inevitably, a Quality System will involve many documents, relating to both the development process and the definition and operation of the System itself. These documents need to be controlled carefully, for instance, to prevent out-of-date documents being used. Also, documents need to be handled consistently, in particular in the way they are issued, controlled and changed. (This will include equivalent information held on computer systems).

The Standard requires that there are procedures to handle documents: to approve, issue and control change and modification. (Often one of the first ✓ procedures established within a Quality System is a "Procedure for Handling Procedures".)

Some other requirements for document control are:

- a re-issue procedure (for example when a certain extent of change has been made);
- withdrawal of obsolete copies;
- availability of documents at essential locations (e.g. programming standards accessible to or issued to the programming teams);
- staff to be nominated with responsibility for updating documents;
- implemented document changes to be recorded.

Inspection and test status

This requirement follows from the need to Inspect and Test; it makes little sense to not know the state of a component or product once it has been tested. A process is needed to identify and record the test status:

(i)   not yet inspected
(ii) inspected – accepted
(iii) inspected – not accepted.

It is somewhat more difficult to make this status apparent on software components, but this can be done, for example, by using comment or textual fields on programs, designs and documentation.

It is important that someone is assigned to be the Inspection authority for releasing "conforming product" – and equally for preventing non-conforming product being released or delivered. For major product releases, this authority would typically be the Quality Manager, while for development components, this should be a Quality Engineer (or equivalent role) assigned to the project.

Purchasing

The Standard requires that anything purchased (equipment, materials, services) is adequate for its purpose, and therefore checked against appropriate defined requirements. There is a three-stage process to purchasing:

  (i)   Specify the requirements for the item or service.
  (ii) Inspect or Verify the requirements are met.
  (iii) Record the performance of the purchased item or service.

This also applies to sub-contractors and sub-contracted personnel.

Purchased items need to be identified (e.g. by a label or identifier) so that it is clear whether they have been inspected or verified and, if so, what the outcome was (accepted, rejected). Where suppliers are used on the basis of their past performance, there must be evidence to substantiate this (i.e. supplier records).

Purchaser-supplied product

This is a requirement which may not be immediately obvious — its origin is in the manufacturing sector, where it is relatively common practice for a customer or purchaser to supply material or a component to be worked on, finished and incorporated into another product. In this case, procedures are needed to ensure that this purchaser-supplied product is suitable and properly controlled; for instance:

- checking that the correct quantity has been received;
- holding and storing the product correctly;
- preventing its use for the wrong job;
- periodically checking for damage.

These requirements are as much to protect the purchaser as the supplier; they ensure that the quality of the final product is not weakened by, for example, the supplier mishandling or misusing the supplied products.

For software, there are parallels; for example, a purchaser may supply an existing application to be upgraded, or a client may supply information as part of an analysis and design task. The equivalent requirements to those stated above would then be:

- checking that the complete application or information had been received;
- saving the application or information properly (e.g. to prevent corruption or to maintain confidentiality);

Support requirements 39

- preventing its use on any other project work or by anyone else not working for this purchaser;
- periodically checking that it is held correctly and is still complete.

Statistical techniques

This requirement applies "where appropriate", indicating that it is not mandatory; however, it is usually interpreted as meaning at least simple defect tracking and trend analysis (e.g. are defects getting more or less frequent and in which components are they occurring most). It is useful to adopt basic statistical (or quantitative) indicators for software products such as failure rates, error densities, fault costs or similar and to evaluate these indicators against targets for achievement or performance. They can be analysed for trends (e.g. decrease with time) as part of the Quality System procedures. Another approach is to introduce a Cost of Quality program to analyse factors such as cost of correction against the costs of improvement.

Quality records

The Standard requires that quality-related records are created and held, and that they are readily accessible and stored for a "defined period", although it does not state what this period is. A guideline is that a supplier's quality records should be retained for as least as long as the product is being maintained or supported.(In some circumstances, where products are being delivered as part of a contract, it may be advisable to obtain legal advice as to how long this period should be.)

Quality records are those which:

- demonstrate achievement of the required quality
- demonstrate operation of the Quality System

and hence include items such as Inspection and Review reports, product fault records, internal quality audits, and sub-contractor performance records.

The purchaser must have access to Quality Records if this has been agreed contractually; the records concerned would normally be identified in the Project Quality Plan.

Training

The Standard requires that the training needs of "all persons affecting quality" are identified, and correspond to the skills and qualifications needed for their work. Records of their training requirements, based on education, skills, qualifications and experience, need to be maintained. In practice, these records will cover everyone contributing to the products and services (i.e. contributing to development), since they all affect product quality to some extent.

For software work, there are as yet few areas where specific qualifications or certificates are essential (unlike some industrial work such as welding). This does not prevent a company adopting qualifications (e.g. a Certificate in SSADM or in the project management methodology PRINCE) as a training requirement within their Quality System – or requiring that all personnel must have attended a particular training course before performing specific project tasks. However, if a company does this, they must ensure that they meet this requirement, otherwise they are in breach of their own Quality System and hence BS 5750/ISO 9001.

Interpreting the standard for software: ISO 9000-3

The BS 5750/ISO 9001 Standard is written in general terms so that it is independent of any particular type of product or service. This can make it difficult to understand for a particular industry, and so a number of Guidance or Interpretation Documents have been developed, including ones for the software sector. These are intended to assist companies to understand and meet the requirements of BS 5750/ISO 9001 so that they can implement a Quality System which is appropriate to their sector, but which still complies with the Standard. These Guides also assist Quality Systems auditors to perform an assessment appropriate to the work being done. (Note that any non-compliances are stated against the full Standard, not the Interpretation Guide.)

In the software sector, the Guidance document ISO 9000-3 is intended to fulfill this purpose. A draft version (DIS 9000-2) is included in the *TickIT Guide* published by the DTI TickIT project (see References). It is worth summarising its approach to illustrate more clearly what a software-based Quality System is likely to contain.

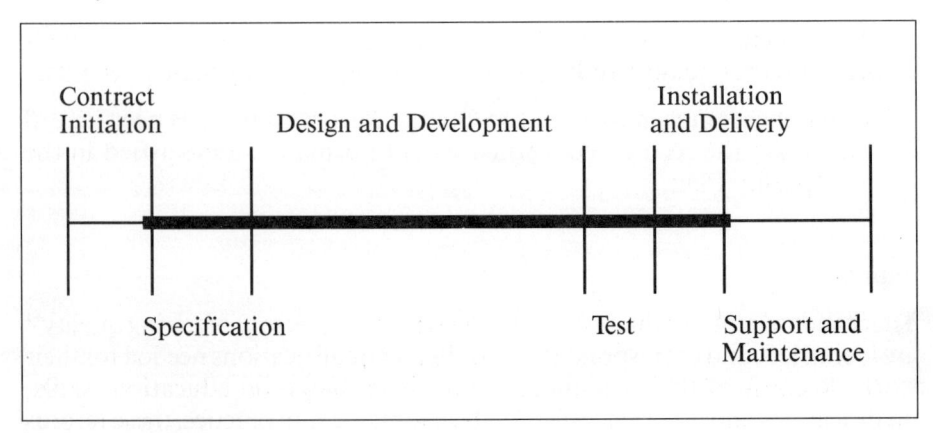

Figure 3.6 A software life-cycle for ISO 9000-3

The ISO 9000-3 Interpretation recognises the software life-cycle as the fundamental feature of the development process (Figure 3.6); all the Quality System elements are integrated around the life-cycle. The Quality System requirements are interpreted as three groups (Figure 3.7):

- The Quality System Framework

    Quality System content, internal audit and corrective action requirements

- Life Cycle Activities

    Requirements based on the project life-cycle

- Supporting Activities

    Requirements relating to project work but independent of particular life-cycle phases (e.g. document control)

ISO 9000-3 Breakdown		
Quality System Framework	Life Cycle Activities	Supporting Activities
Management responsibility Quality System Internal Quality System Audit Corrective Action	Contract Review Purchaser's Requirements Specification Development Planning Quality Planning Design and Implementation Testing and Validation Acceptance Maintenance	Configuration Management Document Control Quality Records Measurements Rules, Practices and Conventions Tools and Techniques Purchasing Included Software Product Training

Figure 3.7 ISO 9000-3 Interpretation of BS 5750/ISO 9001

The Quality System Framework

The breakdown of requirements (elements) within the Quality System Framework is:

- Management Responsibility

    (including both supplier and purchaser and the performance of regular joint project reviews)

- Quality System

    (including preparation of a supplier quality plan for development work)

- Internal Quality System Audits

42   *Standards for quality systems: BS 5750/ISO 9000*

- Corrective Action

    (including investigating causes of process problems and product defects)

Statistics on queries received

Life Cycle Activities

Life-cycle activities are identified as:

- Contract Review

- Purchaser's Requirements Specification

- Development Planning

    (i.e. a complete phase-by-phase definition of the project and its content)

- Quality Planning

    (definition and execution of a Project Quality Plan)

- Design and Implementation

    (including definition of methods, practices and reviews)

- Testing and Validation

    (specific test planning is required)

- Acceptance

    (including definition of the means of delivery and installation)

- Maintenance

    (as previously agreed by purchaser and supplier; records must be maintained)

Supporting Activities

Supporting Activities are:

- Configuration Management

    (identifying, controlling and tracking software and documentation)

- Document Control

    (control of project and Quality System documents)

- Quality Records

    (covering both the products and performance of the Quality System)

- Measurements

    (recording and analysing operational product defects and indicating development progress — ideally a programme of product and development metrics)

- Rules, Practices and Conventions

    (including review of their effectiveness)

- Tools and Techniques

    (technical and management)

- Purchasing

    (including sub-contracted work)

- Included Software Product

    (where products or components are provided by the purchaser or other external source)

- Training

    relevant to the life-cycle methods and tools, and possibly to the application area of the software)

This guidance document therefore indicates that these are the types of activity expected in a software developer's Quality System in order for it to comply with BS 5750 Part 1/ISO 9001 requirements.

Quality System Elements

The *TickIT Guide* also indicates what each Quality System element requires in terms of:

- Activity Definition

    (what activity the company must perform to satisfy the requirement)

- Objectives and Criteria

    (what the activity will achieve and how will its success be demonstrated)

- Outputs

    (normally resulting from the activity)

- Standards and Procedures

    (applicable to the activity)

- Control Mechanisms

    (to evaluate the outcome or outputs)

- Approvals

    (to indicate that the outcome has met the criteria for the activity)

When done for each Quality System requirement, it provides a precise definition of how each requirement will be met by the organisation's specific Quality System. This method is suggested for consideration by any organisation implementing its own Quality System, using this structure as a basis.

Summary

The BS 5750/ISO 9001 Standard provides a comprehensive definition of what an organisation's Quality System should contain. It can be used as a 'formula' when an organisation constructs its own Quality System. For software work, this Quality System needs to be built on a set of project life-cycle and supporting activities and procedures. Its overall aim is to ensure that a minimum reasonable set of controls are in place on working practice to produce an acceptable product for the purchaser.

4
Working practices: Procedures, standards and codes of practice

Documented working practices

One of the fundamental requirements of a Quality System is that the working practices and processes by which the product is produced or the service is provided are written down. There are a number of reasons why:

- to define the normal, proven, way of doing the work;
- for consistency of practice, since everyone doing the same work follows the same procedure;
- to shorten learning time for anyone unfamiliar with the work;
- to allow the work process to be evaluated and assessed (both for internal personnel looking to improve or correct work processes and external personnel assessing work practices, e.g. against BS 5750);
- to ensure authorities and responsibilities for the work process and its checking (quality control) are clear.

Once the procedures have been written and established, an organisation has a complete definition of its working practices and, in effect, its expertise. This set of definitions is valuable, not only because of the time and effort that has been spent in creating it but because it defines exactly how the organisation does its work — the written procedures record its own 'house style'. This may mean that the documentation has to be treated as commercially sensitive, since it documents the organisational expertise built up with experience over time, and therefore may represent a substantial commercial advantage over competitors. Properly structured Quality System documentation can allow a sensible level of commercial confidentiality, principally by separation of the organisational information in the Quality Manual, Procedures and Standards into their own Manuals and project information in Quality Plans.

Documenting a work process does not require that the process is the best possible, nor does it restrict the process to being performed only in this way if some variation is justified for a particular project or work task. In setting up the Quality System, it may have been a substantial effort in the first place to get the process adequately defined and documented, with discrepancies and problems being found. The principal requirement for a Quality System is that the documented process is understandable and workable — improvement can always follow once the procedure is established and being followed consistently.

Variations on documented Procedures are allowable provided that, in advance, these variations are defined, explained and authorised; for example, by the Project Manager within the Project Quality Plan and approved by the Quality Manager.

How to document working practice

There are various ways of defining working practice, represented by terms such as Procedure, Standard, Code of Practice, Work Instruction and Guide. While these terms are not always used consistently, together they represent two types of practice: mandatory and optional.

Mandatory documents

Mandatory documents are usually termed Procedures, Standards or Work Instructions. A Procedure is the definition of a work process, normally written as a sequence of steps to be followed. It must be sufficiently explanatory to be understood by personnel learning to do the work, but should not be unnecessarily detailed or complicated for those already familiar with the work (it should not 'talk down' to the regular practitioners). A Procedure explains, as necessary for each step of the particular work process: **what, how, when, where, by whom**.

Typically, there will be a Procedure for each work process or technique — for software development, this usually means for each life-cycle stage (Requirements, Design, Programming, etc.) and for each supporting process (Change Control, Project Review, etc.). Every work task and operation performed within the Quality System needs to be covered by or referenced to some form of documented Procedure. A Procedure can reference others; sometimes a hierarchy of Procedures and 'Sub-Procedures' is used, to cover both the basic process and the detailed steps within it.

A Standard is a mandatory set of rules for a product or process — in software, one of the most common examples is a Programming Standard. Perhaps the clearest distinction between Procedures and Standards is that, by following a Procedure, a Standard should automatically be achieved, e.g. Design Procedures which achieve the Design Standards for the documented design outputs. Procedures can themselves be looked on as Standards in that they are mandatory, i.e. the rule is that they are always followed unless an alternative is specifically defined and authorised. If necessary, there can be alternative ways of achieving a Standard, e.g. different documentation methods to achieve a Document Standard.

A Work Instruction can be used to provide a more detailed form of Procedure which can be used, for example, to define more precisely a particular procedural step. Another use is to define the precise content of a project work task where alternatives are possible or no defined procedure exists. Work Instructions can be used to give flexibility of working, but must be properly authorised at the time of application, and like Procedures must be treated as mandatory when called up for a work task. For software work, examples of Work Instructions include how to perform specific steps of a Program Testing task or a specific method of interviewing users within a Systems Analysis task.

Advisory documents

Codes of Practice and Guides provide supplementary, advisory, information for the mandatory Procedures and Standards. They may include, for example, the 'hints and tips' which help programmers work to a Procedure or Standard and include examples of what it is intended to achieve. The information is advisory and sometimes viewed as 'best recommended practice'. It is the 'Highway Code' for the work processes — while not mandatory, it is inadvisable to ignore it, and you may have to explain why you have if things go wrong.

Within a Quality System, Procedures and Standards (and Work Instructions where needed) are vital. They must cover all the work practices used, and be authorised, identified and applied, usually by means of a Quality Plan. They must be accurate and up-to-date (this itself needs a Procedure for updating and re-issuing them). It is recommended to apply these same processes to the advisory documents such as Guides and Codes of Practice, but the same rigour of content and application will not always be necessary (See Figure 4.1 for summary).

Structure and content of procedures

It is strongly recommended to establish a common format and structure for the Procedures and Standards (and to apply it to the advisory documentation as well). A sample structure for a Procedure is described below, although it could apply to any similar document (Standard, Code of Practice, etc.). The main headings are:

48   *Working practices: Procedures, standards and codes of practice*

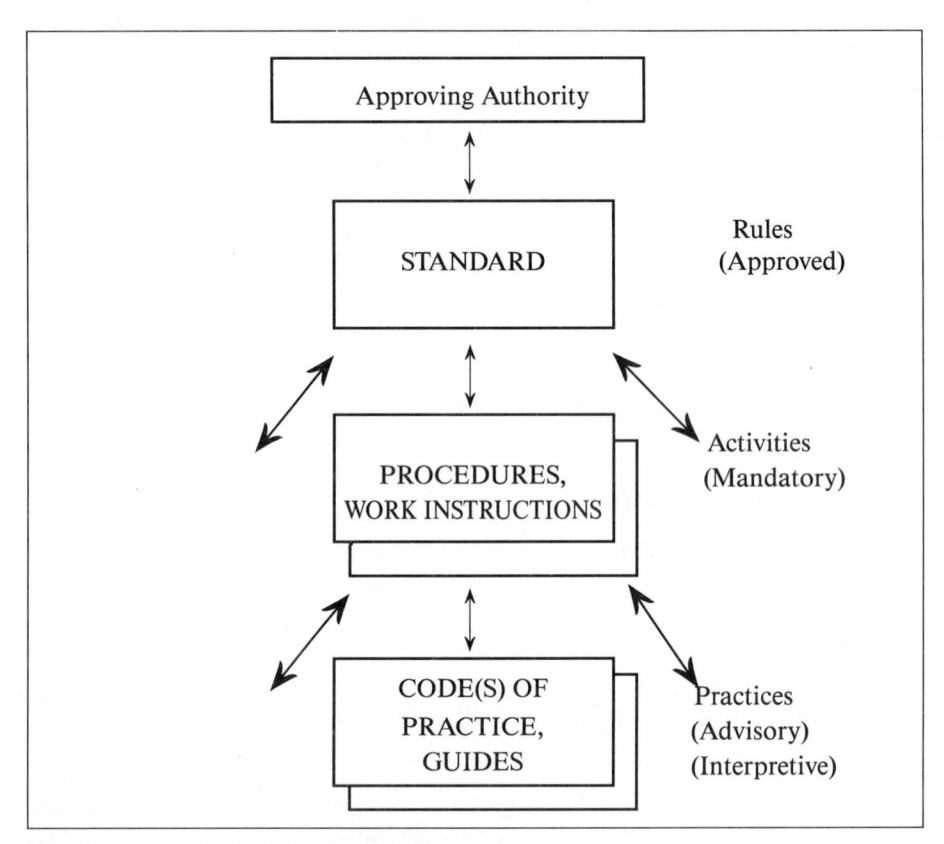

Figure 4.1   Documenting Working Practice

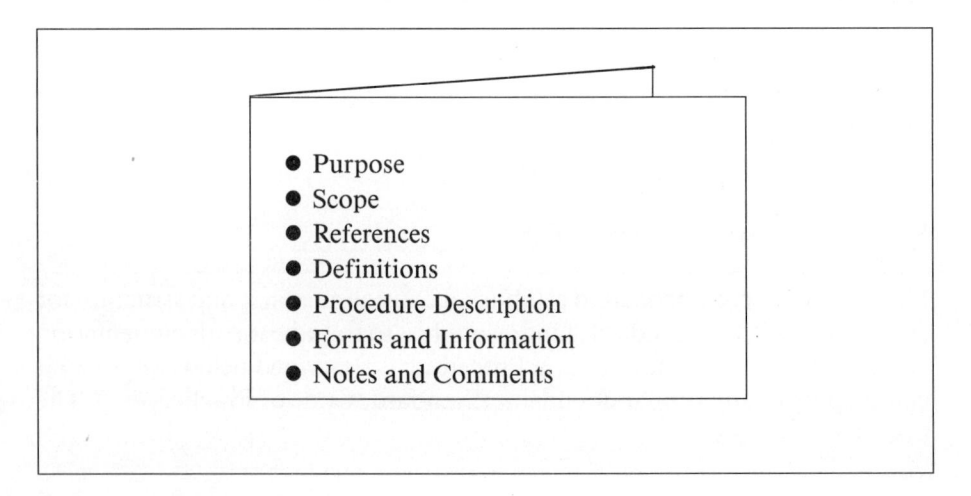

Figure 4.2   Procedure contents

Purpose

The purpose of the document is stated, to make it clear to which work task, method or practice it applies and what it is intended to achieve. A short summary of the Procedure will be helpful at this point, if only to confirm that the user is looking at the right one.

Scope

The scope of application of the Procedure is defined, including to what types of activity, which parts of the organisation, the extent to which it is mandatory and when it is applicable. This section avoids someone having to read the procedure to find out if it applies to their work, as well as making it clear under what circumstances it applies.

References

This identifies any other documents (e.g. Procedures, Standards, Guides, internal and external) to which reference is made or which apply to the document. For example, the Documentation Standard which applies to the Procedure should be referenced here, also any procedures which are referenced from the body of the text. This makes it easy to identify what other documents may be needed to understand or carry out this Procedure.

Definitions

Terms used within the document, particularly any which are specialist and/or local to the Procedure, should be defined here; this should also include any terms which are likely to be misunderstood.

Description (the procedure itself)

This is the description of the Procedure itself, written as a series of short steps, preferably with each paragraph numbered for easy reference and to assist understanding and compliance. Diagrams (e.g. flow-charts) can be used if these improve clarity (but try to avoid or minimise duplication of textual and diagrammatic information to prevent inconsistency).

For a Standard or similar document which does not have a natural sequence to its content (e.g. a collection of rules or requirements), each paragraph should still be numbered to help indicate its structure.

One of the skills of writing a procedure is achieving the right balance between formality and effectiveness. The clarity with which the procedure is described matters most to the personnel who use it and therefore it must be written in 'plain language' and reviewed with them to ensure it is clearly understood; the information preceding the description ensures that the procedure is applied in the right circumstances and that its relevance of application can be verified, externally if necessary.

Forms and information

When a Procedure uses or generates information, and particularly if it has a defined format (e.g. content and layout of a form or data record), it can be defined or illustrated here. It should be clear whether the format is mandatory.

Notes and comments

It can be helpful to include supplementary information such as the background to the technique being described or working examples of the Procedure's application, as guidance to the user. It must be clear whether this information is an example and whether it is mandatory. (Alternatively, this information can be provided as a separate Guide.)

Identification

Every Procedure must be uniquely identified and authorised, typically by means of a front sheet which states its Title, Reference (or Identification) Number, Revision Status (e.g. Draft/Issued, Version no.), Authorisation and Amendment Record. Authorisation is normally by the person responsible for the process defined in the Procedure (e.g. Senior Engineer, Project Manager, Support Manager) to indicate its acceptability for its purpose, and by the Quality Manager to indicate its acceptability within the Quality System. This authorisation process will itself be part of a Procedure.

What procedures and standards are needed?

A typical structure of the documentation set for Procedures and Standards is described below. This structure should both meet the requirements of a BS 5750/ISO 9001 Quality System and provide the flexibility for the documentation to be added to, amended or withdrawn as circumstances require. Note that other ways of organising and structuring the documentation set are possible; the main requirements for a Quality System are that the documents are controlled, available for use, and removed when obsolete.

Identification standard

The first document is a Standard defining the identification and numbering system to be applied to all documents within the Quality System, for example:

What procedures and standards are needed? 51

XYZ-ABC-DOC-nnn

where XYZ identifies the company, ABC the department or project (as relevant), DOC the type of document (Procedure, Standard etc.) and nnn is its number within the documentation set. (The identifier is intended to define which document it is, where it belongs in the Quality System, and what is its scope or application.) The identifier of this particular (company-wide) document Standard would be XYZ-STD-001.

It is useful to use the same identification system for project documents.

This Standard should identify who controls and validates the issue of identifiers (e.g. QA personnel, Documentation Librarian), since each identifier must be unique and follow the Standard. The current set of identifiers for Quality System documents is maintained in a Procedures Index or Documentation Register (a master list which records the current revision of documents is a requirement of BS 5750).

An additional practice can be to include a suffix to indicate the issue and status of the document: e.g. XYZ-STD-001/A means draft A of this document, XYZ-STD-001/2 means issue 2.

Procedure standard

The next document (XYZ-STD-002 in the format adopted here) defines the requirements for the style, format and structure of the Procedures and Standards documents. This is the 'Standard for Standards and Procedures'. It is worthwhile indicating if any flexibility in these requirements is allowed (i.e. for a procedure applicable internally within a project).

Implementation procedure

Document XYZ-PROC-003 is the Procedure for initiating, developing, approving and issuing Procedures and Standards – the 'Procedure for Generating Procedures'.

This procedure is essential within a Quality System in order to demonstrate control over the definition of working practices. A typical approach is to place the responsibility for identifying the need for a procedure with the manager responsible for the work area or discipline, e.g. the Development Manager, and for its development to be agreed by the appropriate discipline head. The procedure is then developed by personnel appointed by the manager of the work area – preferably those who are experienced in the work process itself. The Quality Manager will need to review and authorise it as suitable for inclusion in the Quality System.

Documentation index

Document XYZ-DOC-004 is an Index or Register of all current Quality System Documentation. This Index will need updating whenever any of these documents is introduced, amended or withdrawn. It may be more convenient to include groups of documents (e.g. Design Procedures) as entries in this Index, with each group having its own sub-index (for instance where the number of procedures involved or their frequency of change makes it difficult to maintain a single comprehensive Index). The key requirement is that the current document set is identified and that its validity of issue and usage can be verified.

Potential documentation (e.g. procedures being written but not yet issued) can be included, as long as their status as being under development is recorded.

Documentation set

The main set of documents are the operational Procedures and Standards and any Guides or Codes of Practice. They must comply with the format and presentation requirements of the XYZ-STD-002 standard described above. The documents can be grouped into whatever sets or manuals are most convenient — for software work it may be useful to start with a breakdown into:

- quality system (i.e QA related, non-technical)
- life-cycle (i.e. project phases, technical)
- supporting (i.e. project-wide, such as project management, change control)

Documentation format

A typical documentation format (as required by the XYZ-STD-002 Standard) is:

Cover page

Information on this page is:
- document identifier
- document title
- issue/revision
- approvals
- document number (i.e. for this copy)
- amendment record (for recording when the document has been updated).

Index page

This is the Index to the document. Each page of the document is identified by a unique number and includes the identification of the document to which it belongs (e.g. in the bottom right-hand corner). One practice is to produce the Index as a 'list of effective pages', indicating each page's current revision status; this means that each page can be checked against the corresponding information in the Index in order to verify that the document is complete and up-to-date, including any amendments.

Procedure pages

A specific format can be defined for these pages if required; this is mainly useful for presentational reasons or to ensure that all necessary content is included. Such content and structure must comply with the relevant requirements of the XYZ-STD-002 standard.

Procedure content

As explained above, the content of the procedure should be clear, concise, and written at the right level of detail both for those who use it and for those who need to familiarise themselves with it. It is recommended to number or label each step (e.g. by numbering sections, paragraphs and sub-paragraphs), so that progress and compliance can be checked easily against each step, and so that a possible problem or non-compliance can be located unambiguously within the procedure. The following is a sample extract from a Systems Analysis Procedure:

"Step 5: User Review of Logical Design

5. Summary; The Logical Design shall be reviewed by the user and approved as suitable for use in the Physical Design Stage.

5.1 The Logical Design documentation shall be reviewed with the User Department Representative(s) nominated in the Project Quality Plan, by means of the Review Procedure XYZ-PROC-012. The Design documentation shall be modified and further reviewed as necessary to resolve any points raised during Review.

5.2 Formal authorisation of the Logical Design being suitable for proceeding to the Physical Design Stage shall be obtained from Representative(s) and Management of the User Department as nominated in the Project Quality Plan. Document XYZ-DOC-005 shall be used for this purpose.

5.3 If required by the Project Quality Plan, a System Audit meeting shall be held.

5.4 A Project Review meeting shall be performed, with attendance as defined in the Project Quality Plan."

Procedures do not have to be in textual form; diagrams such as a flow-chart of steps can be used for relevant sections, particularly where alternative paths through the procedure are possible. If this is done, each step should be labelled in the same way as for a textual paragraph.

What a procedure should tell us

Each procedure should provide the following information about the work process it is defining:

- What is the process?
- What does it produce or achieve, and what criteria can be applied to verify the outcome?
- What outputs are produced?
- What Standards or other Procedures apply?
- What process is used to verify the outcome?
- Who approves the outputs and/or outcome?

Use of the imperative

In a mandatory document such as a Procedure or Standard it is recommended to use the words "shall" and "must", rather than words such as "should" or "usually" which could be interpreted as implying that the content is optional; Guidance and other optional documents are recommended to use the latter tenses.

Standards content

Standards should be organised in the same way as Procedures, and belong to the same Quality System documentation set. It is helpful to think of Standards as being a set of rules, which are achieved by adherence to a related procedure. They are particularly useful in defining requirements for products such as documents or the particular usage of techniques, methods or tools to implement or support working practice.

To be useable, Standards must be written in a form which is verifiable – in fact the verification requirements can be written into the Standard itself. BS 5750/ ISO 9001 is a good example of a verifiable external Standard (note that not all externally available Standards are written so as to be verifiable – see Appendix 4).

Codes of practice

It is recommended to treat a Code of Practice as an 'advisory' procedure or standard, so that it can be adopted as mandatory if required. It is best structured in the same way. If it complements an existing standard (e.g. by providing more detail), this should be clear in the information provided.

Work instructions

As in the case of procedures, BS 5750 does not specify a particular format for Work Instructions, but they must meet the same requirements as procedures of authorisation and proof of implementation. Because an Instruction may be raised as a 'one-off' for a particular work task, it may not be possible to adhere completely to the same requirements for procedures, but it should still identify:

- its purpose and scope of application;
- its author and approval for application;
- whether it replaces an existing procedure or procedure step (or previous instruction);
- the work process itself.

When short 'one-off' Work Instructions are raised frequently, a standard form is helpful.

BS 5750/ISO 9001 requirements

The exact set of Standards and Procedures within a Quality System are the choice of the organisation, but the BS 5750/ISO 9001 Standard indicates which elements of the Quality System are required to be covered by documented Standards, Procedures or Instructions; this can be looked on as minimum requirements for the set of Standards and Procedures.

BS 5750/ISO 9001 states a general requirement to prepare documented 'procedures and instructions' for the Quality System and to implement them effectively. For software work, it is helpful to group them as Quality Management, Technical, and Support-related. The following is based on those mentioned explicitly by the Standard:

Quality Management

- Internal Quality Audits (including follow-up).
- Corrective Action.

56 Working practices: Procedures, standards and codes of practice

Technical (Project-related)

- Contract Review.
- Standards of acceptability for product features and requirements.
- Design Control (including product verification).
- Design Changes (including review and approval).
- Process Control (Work Instructions and Standards).
- Purchaser-Supplied Product (verification, storage and maintenance).
- Inspection and Testing (Receiving, In-process and Final).
- Control of Non-Conforming Product (including review and rework).
- Inspection, Measuring and Test Equipment.
- Product Handling, Storage, Packaging and Delivery.
- Servicing.

Support

- Document Control (including approval, issue and identification).
- Quality Records.
- Product Identification and Traceability.
- Statistical Techniques (i.e. some level of verification of process capability and product effectiveness).
- Training (in particular identifying training needs).

It is helpful to cross-reference the set of Standards and Procedures to correspond with each requirement of BS 5750/ISO 9001. This helps to ensure that each BS 5750 requirement is met, and indicates how the particular set of Standards and Procedures match the BS 5750 requirements, which makes it easier to audit the Quality System.

A documentation set for software development

The life-cycle structure of software development work means that it is not always convenient to group the set of Procedures and Standards in the same way as the BS 5750/ISO 9001 Standard. In practice, the following documentation set would be typical:

Quality system (general)

This documentation sub-set covers general, project independent, activities.

Quality Manual.

- Quality Policy and Objectives.
- Organisation.
- Description of the overall Quality System.
- Procedures Index.
- Quality System Review and Audit; planning, selection, conduct, presentation of results and follow-up.
- Quality System Improvement; collection and analysis of quality-related information (e.g. client/user satisfaction survey).
- Procurement; purchasing and accounting, supplier and contractor evaluation and monitoring, inspection and handling of externally supplied items.
- Training Procedures; recruitment, training needs analysis, career progression, performance appraisal.

Quality system (project-related)

This documentation sub-set covers practices applicable at some or all project stages.

- Quality Plan Standards; planning procedures, contents definition and approval procedures.
- Review Procedures; conduct and content of reviews, identification of attendees, reporting and follow-up, and use of checklists.
- Documentation Standards, including style, layout, approval and distribution, version and change control.
- Configuration Management procedures, covering item identification, release, version control, change control, handling of non-conformances.
- Backup, Security and Archiving; including both software and documentation (and associated hardware if relevant).
- Progress Reporting and Monitoring; covering project planning, monitoring and reporting and progress review.
- Non-conforming (defective) Items; usually covered within development and maintenance procedures (how to handle non-conforming items to limit the impact on the products).

58   Working practices: Procedures, standards and codes of practice

- Corrective Action; usually covered within development procedures, but sometimes as specific product or document modification procedures.

Quality system (project specific)

This documentation sub-set applies to specific project stages:

- User Requirements Specification; specification review procedure (including customer/purchaser contact and discussions).
- Contract/Project Proposal; proposal standards and preparation and approval procedures.
- Project Initiation; proposal acceptance and project start-up procedures.
- Requirements Specification; requirements and functional specification standards, analysis procedures.
- High-level Design; system design standards, methods and tools procedures and guidance, design verification procedures and standards (including formal review/inspection).
- Detailed Design; technical design standards, methods and tools procedures and guidance, verification procedures and standards (including design walkthroughs, review and inspection).
- Code and Unit Test; programming procedures and standards, code walkthrough and unit testing and review procedures.
- Integration and System Test; build and integration procedures and guidelines, system testing procedures and standards, fault logging and analysis procedures.
- Acceptance Test; acceptance test procedures and standards.
- Replication; copying and verification procedures.
- Handover/Release; handover and release procedures.
- Storage and Shipment; product handling procedures marking, handling, packing, delivery, etc.).
- Delivery and Installation; delivery procedure, installation planning and performance standards.
- User Training; User Manual standards, course development standards and training procedures.
- Maintenance; maintenance and support, fault logging and analysis, change control and release procedures, service level agreements.

It must be emphasised that this is a sample set of Procedures and Standards to illustrate what a documentation set might consist of and how it can be organised; other equivalents or variations are possible. The main reason for variation is because of the particular development life-cycle used.

Individual copies of a document need only be issued to those who implement the procedure or comply with a standard. Some procedures may be no more than a page of content in a simple case, while others may need to define detailed circumstances and therefore be more substantial. Lengthy or excessively detailed Quality System documents should be avoided (can the detailed information be contained in a separate Procedure Guide instead?).

External standards and guidance

Obviously, it is going to be a substantial task to produce a completely documented set of procedures and standards, even if most of them are reasonably brief. It is tempting to look to external sources for existing Standards or Procedures to adopt or (more realistically) use as a basis for a company's requirements. Unfortunately, there are comparatively few such documents available in the public domain. Those that are, fall into categories such as:

- Quality System Standards.
- Documentation Standards.
- Guidance and Interpretation Documents related to Standards.
- Technical Standards.
- Sample Procedure and Documentation sets.

and are published by a variety of national and international standards organisations, professional and trade organisations and government departments (particularly Defence). The most common sources are British, European and American Standards bodies and the International Standards Organisation (ISO). Appendix 4 of this book identifies and summarises a selection of such documents which are software-specific or can be applied to software.

5
Quality control: Inspection, review and testing

Introduction

A Quality System must include a substantial element of Quality Control, i.e. checking that the components, products and other outputs meet their requirements and are free from defect. In the past, software work has been weak in this respect, tending to concentrate on the testing of completed executable programs (and hence at a late stage in the development life-cycle), with little checking of earlier design work, or of the associated documentation.

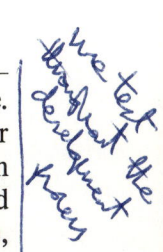

The BS 5750/ISO 9001 Standard requires comprehensive quality control of the product while it is being developed, and proper measures for products found to be unsatisfactory; additionally, it requires attention to why deficiencies occur and the instigation and monitoring of corrective action. This action includes both the products themselves and, if necessary, the processes used (e.g. changing design procedures or techniques).

Aspects of design and development work within a Quality System which are related to quality control or verification work include:

- preparation of quality plans which include verification requirements;
- identification of the controls and skills needed to achieve product quality;
- compatibility of inspection and test procedures with the design and development processes (i.e. for software, with the life-cycle model);
- definition of the responsibility, authority and relationship of personnel performing verification;
- provision of adequate resources and trained personnel for verification;
- review of requirements for adequacy and resolution where they are incomplete, ambiguous or conflicting;
- procedures to verify product design against requirements;

62   Quality control: Inspection, review and testing

- designs will either include or reference acceptance criteria;
- verification that design outputs correspond to the design stage inputs;
- verification that purchased product (components) meet their specifications;
- verification of purchaser-supplied products (components);
- monitoring of processes and products during development;
- maintenance of Inspection and Test records;
- providing evidence that the completed product conforms to its requirements.

In addition, there are detailed requirements for Inspection and Testing during development. These are described below.

Inspection and test

One of the principal requirements of BS 5750/ISO 9001 is for effective Inspection and Test during design and development. The Standard recognises several stages to Inspection and Test:

- Receiving: "incoming product" must be assessed to verify that it meets its requirements. Hence any input to the development process such as existing software designs, user data, etc. must be checked against requirements which reflect its use in the project.
- In-process: products must be inspected or tested during their development according to a quality plan, project test plan or equivalent, which contains or references documented procedures for this process.
- Final: products must be inspected and tested to show that the product conforms to its requirements; also to show that all the earlier tests (receiving and in-process) have been performed successfully.

How much quality control?

It is important to realise that the Standard does not define directly the level or extent of verification or Quality Control that is needed for a product. However, what is appropriate can be inferred from a number of other requirements of the Standard:

- design outputs must meet design input requirements (i.e. inspection and testing should show this);

Inspection and test 63

- the design input requirements are defined, documented and adequate (e.g. no incomplete, ambiguous or conflicting requirements);
- acceptance criteria are stated or referenced;
- any regulatory requirements relevant to the product are met;
- characteristics that are crucial to the "safe and proper functioning" of the product are identified (and hence demonstrated).

With a number of specific exceptions, verification can be performed by the development or operational areas (i.e. it does not have to be a task for a separate QA department), although independent involvement is important. The means of verification (e.g. design reviews, demonstrations) should be defined, usually in a Project Quality Plan, including identification of who participates and their role and their required competence (e.g. experience, qualifications and role).

Records

The Standard requires that records of Inspection and Testing are created and held as part of a set of project Quality Records. These records provide evidence of product testing to show it has been done (and to what extent), and allow the effectiveness of the Inspection and Testing elements of the Quality System to be evaluated from the accumulated project information.

Handling of defects

Another requirement of verification is proper handling of defects and the defective products — otherwise, it undermines the benefits of the verification activities. BS 5750/ISO 9001 requires that the test status of a product (and the result of testing) is clear, by means of some form of identification on the product, and/or by associated test records. Some relevant practices are:

- indicating on the product (e.g. program listing, design diagram) whether it has been verified (and what the outcome was e.g. pass/fail);
- maintaining records of the verification of all components, products and documents, and the outcome;
- requiring that products are signed-off before release to the customer or for subsequent project work; there must be an appropriate verification authority (e.g Technical Manager, Team Leader) to do this.

When a product fails verification (becomes a "non-conforming product"), there must be a method of deciding what action is to be taken, e.g:

- rework to correct the defect;

- acceptance without rework (with the defect and its effect defined and accepted by the next user or the customer);
- partial rework (i.e. of defined defects) and/or partial acceptance;
- rejection of product requiring total rework (e.g. new design solution required).

A reworked product must be re-verified sufficiently to ensure that the defect has been removed and that no others have been introduced. As a minimum, this means it must be signed-off by the 'verification authority' to confirm that it has been corrected — where the change is extensive or significant, a full verification should be repeated.

Verification activities

Running through the various BS 5750/ISO 9001 requirements is the need for a range of verification activities:

- inspection, testing and monitoring;
- design reviews and audits;
- statement of verification requirements, including resources and personnel (e.g. as a Project Test Plan);
- responsibilities, including the use of independent personnel for design reviews and audits.

Appropriate types of verification activity must cover the entire product development process (development life-cycle). Hence each phase of a software project should include suitable Inspection, Review or Test activities, with identification of who participates, what process is followed, what products are verified and how the outcome (particularly defects and corrective action) is handled. If preferred, this can be done within a separate Test Plan (or Verification, Validation and Test Plan).

Reviews and audits — what are they?

The software industry has many names for evaluation techniques; for example, Design Reviews, Audits, Technical Reviews, Inspections, Walkthroughs. Some of these are management techniques, to assess, for example, progress against the project plan, while some are technical, such as examination of a document to detect defects and problems. BS 5750/ISO 9001 requires performance of design reviews and audits in addition to the inspection, test and monitoring processes.

Levels of control

One of the objectives of a Quality System is to achieve effective control over the design and development process — while this is intended to ensure adequate quality of product, this objective inevitably overlaps into the need for management and technical controls. The following summary of Reviews, Audits and Inspections reflects the need for effective quality, technical and management controls during project work, alongside a minimum reasonable number of verification events.

There are three levels of control that can be applied:

- self evaluation; the author of the product (designer, programmer, etc.) evaluates his or her own work product;
- peer evaluation; a technically equivalent, but independent person ('peer') evaluates the product, usually in conjunction with the author;
- external evaluation; someone organisationally or financially independent (e.g. from outside the project or outside the company) evaluates the product.

Within each of these categories, various types and levels of evaluation are possible.

Self evaluation, while better than none at all, is likely to be the least effective — the designer or programmer tends to not see defects he has made, and therefore it is unlikely that an adequate evaluation will be made. There may be little evidence that the evaluation has taken place, or that sufficient time and effort has been spent on it. Most recognised forms of Review include at least one independent person, in a peer or independent role.

If an evaluation event includes someone who is technically or managerially separated, then it is a Review. A technically separated person is independent of the created product and also, preferably, of the performance or outcome of the project. This should be someone not involved in the project or team (or at least a colleague who is not working on the same project task). Examples of 'technically separated' review techniques are Design Reviews, Technical Reviews, Inspections and Walkthroughs. They precede or complement testing activities which, equally, should have a significant technically independent evaluation element, such as review of the test plan and data.

Audits

Audit is an external evaluation, conducted by a fully independent person or group who is financially separated from the project or organisation being evaluated (and so the outcome of the audit is seen not to be biased by commercial or project pressures). An audit is formal and performed in a manner that ensures credibility, particularly for those affected by its conclusions. An audit, therefore, needs personnel trained as auditors who are following a defined audit process.

Audit conclusions must be based on tangible evidence (e.g. compliance to procedures, achievement of requirements), so that someone else following the same audit process would produce the same evidence and conclusions.

Large organisations may be able to establish their own body of quality or technical auditors (preferably as a part-time role shared with normal project or operational work); smaller organisations may need to employ outside personnel (e.g. qualified consultants) to perform specific audits.

What audits are needed?

There are particular points within a project when audit is useful, taking advantage of the independence of the personnel doing the evaluation and hence the weight that the audit conclusions should have. Examples of project-specific audits are:

- Functional Audits; an implemented product (what *does* it do?) is compared with its requirements specification (what *should* it do?).
- Physical Audits; representations of the product are compared for consistency (are they all the same?). For example, code listings with documentation, or test input data with test specifications.
- In-process Audits; the outcome of a stage of development is evaluated to ensure that the development is consistent and that the products are evolving correctly from the previous stage.

Project-specific audit is valuable where systematic, specific evidence is necessary: for example, the purchaser wants confidence that the developer is producing a technically sound product and/or that progress is genuinely proceeding according to plan. Also, it can find where any weaknesses exist while development is proceeding and there is still time for corrective action to be taken.

Another form of audit is Quality System Audit, which is essential within a BS 5750/ISO 9001 Quality System. Two types of evaluation by audit are required; internal and external. Internal 'first party' Quality System Audits are carried out by (or on behalf of) the senior management (often by the Quality Manager) to evaluate the following:

- that the Quality System satisfies the requirements of BS 5750 (if this is an objective) and the internal company requirements expressed in the Quality Manual;

- that the Quality System is suitable and effective for the organisation's requirements;
 - that follow-up actions from previous audits have been performed.

Normally, a programme of individual internal audits is planned which over a period of 6 or 12 months covers all aspects of the Quality System. Both horizontal audits (e.g. documentation practice on various projects) and vertical audits (e.g. all aspects of an individual project) can be included. There must be a specific, recorded, Management Review of this cycle of internal audits at least annually.

Quality system assessment and registration

External Quality System Audit is the means of formally assessing an organisation's Quality System against the requirements of BS 5750/ISO 9001, leading to the formal Registration of the organisation if successful. This is performed by an external 'third-party' Certification Body, such as the British Standards Institution (BSI), using their own team of assessors. This audit includes examination of the documented Quality Manual and Procedures, and an on-site evaluation of the day-to-day operation of the Quality System, for example by examining quality records, interviewing personnel working within the Quality System and witnessing its operation. Evidence of effective internal (first-party) audit is essential.

Some purchasing organisations (in particular the Ministry of Defence) perform similar 'second-party' assessments of an organisation's Quality System, against either BS 5750/ISO 9001 or similar military NATO standards such as AQAP 1 and 13. This form of assessment is now being phased out in favour of third-party assessment as described above, which will be recognised by all purchasers.

What project reviews are needed?

The majority of software evaluations fall into the review category. These can be further categorised as:

 - management: evaluation against a management or project plan (e.g. to produce a progress report);
 - technical: evaluation of a product (or process) against requirements (or procedure).

Information from technical reviews is in turn fed into management reviews, since the former provide the 'first-hand' evidence of progress in terms of completion of work items and any defects. This information provides the best grounds for management evaluation of project progress against plan.

68   *Quality control: Inspection, review and testing*

When a project is organised around a software life-cycle, the basic rule is that each phase must undergo an appropriate level of review to determine whether it has been completed – if the phase has produced several outputs (e.g. Software Specification and Test Specification), then each has a specific technical review, followed by a single end-of-phase management (project progress) review. For smaller projects, or where there is only one output, it may be possible to have a combined review meeting, with both the appropriate technical and management personnel attending.

Each output or product from individual work tasks within a project stage should undergo some form of evaluation, typically by a peer review technique such as Inspection (the simplest form is a two-person 'desk-check'). As a minimum, the verification 'authority' (e.g. team leader for a designer) should examine and sign-off the product.

Project-level reviews

The US Standard ANSI/IEEE Std 730-1984 for Software Quality Assurance Plans calls for the following project-level reviews on a development project:

– Software Requirements Review
– Preliminary Design Review
– Critical Design Review
– Software Verification Review.

(Critical Design Review is when design work has been completed – it is important from a management point of view since it represents the last opportunity to review the project before the majority of project resources and cost are committed to the subsequent phases.)

The inspection process

The Quality Control or evaluation process for software known as Inspection was originated by Michael Fagan at IBM in the mid-1970s. A detailed description was published in the IBM Systems Journal in 1976 (Vol 15 No.3 pp 182-211) and in various papers and publications since.

As developed at IBM, the method is highly formal, and can be difficult to practise outside a large, well organised company such as IBM. Consequently, many somewhat less formal but more practical versions have been introduced elsewhere. This section describes a typical version of Fagan Inspection, retaining the basic features and benefits of the full method, but with what, for most organisations, will be a more workable level of formality.

Tailored versions of this method can be used for management and technical reviews; an example is described later in this chapter.

The aims of inspection

The principal aim of Fagan Inspection is:

to analyse a product or document to detect defects in it

However, it must be recognised that Inspection cannot be guaranteed to find all defects in the product. Inspection is particularly relevant to the earlier stages of development when the main products are documentation such as Requirements Specifications, Designs, Test Plans, etc. Another key point about Inspection is that all attending recognise that it is an independent evaluation of the product — not a test of the abilities (or shortcomings!) of the author(s) of the product.

Inspection is a form of peer review, where a designer's work is examined by another designer, or an analyst's work by another analyst. It follows a pre-defined procedure which includes steps of individual preparation, performance of the meeting and follow-up of defects and problems. The meeting itself is a controlled and structured discussion, intended to last no more than two hours (and preferably only one hour).

Inspection techniques have been found to be very beneficial in almost all cases when introduced — the potential savings from finding errors early in the life cycle are considerable (they can be introduced ahead of a full Quality System as an additional form of verification). However, they require proper training of personnel and full support from management for the time and cost of their introduction and for their continued performance.

Conditions for success and the benefits

There are many benefits to be achieved from Inspection, provided that its basic rules are followed:

- it can be used before testing of software is possible;
- it detects defects early in the development life cycle;
- it raises the quality of products by detecting more defects and problems than would otherwise be detected;
- it improves project productivity by finding defects when they are easier and cheaper to correct (compared to when found later in the life cycle);
- there will be useful spin-off from group discussion (e.g. making use of the experience of the peer reviewer).

It must be remembered that Inspection cannot be expected to detect all defects and problems in a product. Even when every known defect has been corrected, other more subtle or complex ones may remain — or there may be other defects which lie outside the scope of the Inspection or the criteria applied at Inspection.

The rules of inspection

Success depends heavily on the personnel involved and the 'atmosphere' of the meeting. It is widely agreed amongst practitioners of Inspection that management must not attend the meeting — it is a technical event, not a management event. The Project Manager (or equivalent) can be informed of the meeting and circulated with its results (just as would be the case for product testing), but has no valid role or presence at the meeting. Only on small projects, where technical and project management tasks may necessarily have to be performed by the same person, might this be unavoidable.

Preparation for the meeting is essential — each participant must have been familiarised with the document to the extent necessary for their role in the meeting. This preparation time should be recognised by management as essential, and the participant must spend it properly — typically up to two or three hours. At the meeting, particular care must be taken to direct comments at the product, and not at its author (even though it may be the author who has made the defect).

A successful inspection

The conditions for success can be summarised as follows:

- participants are fully prepared;
- problems are indicated (not necessarily solved);
- conversation is 'frank but friendly';
- technical content, not style, is discussed;
- the product is criticised, not the author;
- management is not present at the meeting;
- it depends heavily on the commitment of team personnel and management.

Why inspection works

According to Fagan, there are two key reasons why Inspection works so well; when an author explains his work to others, he recognises inconsistencies and defects himself, and since the Inspector or Inspection team has an independent viewpoint, different (and perhaps more basic) questions are asked about the product than the author would.

Personnel roles

Inspection is based on group discussion, with specific, defined roles allocated to the personnel attending. A typical set of roles are:

- Moderator
- Author (of the design/program/document, etc.)
- Peer Reviewer
- Customer/User
- Quality Assurance.

The minimum roles necessary are Author and Reviewer (e.g. for 'desk-checking' the output of a work-task within a project phase); as soon as more roles or personnel are involved, or the product has external importance, a moderator should be included.

The Moderator is the chairman and co-ordinator of the entire Inspection process, and is responsible for the progression and conduct of the meeting, although obviously the full support of the participants is necessary for this to be possible. A suitable person for the role is a Team Leader or Senior Analyst who is not involved with the project but who has a recognised technical background and organisational abilities, but not the Project Manager!

The basis of judging the selection of the Moderator, and when one is required, is best defined in the Project Quality Plan or Quality Standards. A Quality Assurance department can advise on and monitor the selection of Moderators. Some organisations identify a 'pool' of Moderators available for Inspection work.

The Author is the person who has developed the item for Inspection and therefore has the greatest knowledge of it (but conversely, the least independent view). If the original Author is not available, a Presenter can be appointed to take this role. During preparation, the Author/Presenter must ensure he or she can fully present and describe the product and is properly prepared to answer questions about it. At the meeting, the Author/Presenter must expect to be actioned to investigate and correct the product afterwards, and to attend a further Inspection if needed.

The Peer Reviewer has the important task of understanding and assessing the product from a technical viewpoint and is in effect the 'expert witness' in resolving suspected defects. The Inspection meeting consists largely of the Author/Presenter explaining the product to the Peer Reviewer. If necessary,

72 Quality control: Inspection, review and testing

separate Peer Reviewers can be appointed to cover different aspects of the product or particular criteria for assessment (e.g. performance or maintenance requirements).

A Customer or User Representative should be considered for participation if they can make a meaningful contribution to the Inspection, such as assessing the product's operating requirements. (Sometimes a separate Inspection for these aspects of the product may be better.) Alternatively, this role can be performed on their behalf by an independent Quality Assurance function or third party who has adequate understanding of their requirements. This should be identified in the Project Quality Plan if applicable.

A Quality Assurance Reviewer can attend Inspections (usually on an optional basis) to assess the effectiveness and compliance of the Inspection against quality procedures and standards. This may sometimes be done as part of an audit of the Quality System. An additional role can be to assess the product against specific quality criteria or requirements. As mentioned above, QA can represent the interests of absent viewpoints such as the customer and/or users.

It is sensible to treat Inspection flexibly, and to invite all those who can reasonably be expected to make a contribution, as long as their role is defined and agreed beforehand. Equally, those invited to attend (preferably on the basis of selection criteria defined in the Quality Plan) should treat their involvement seriously, and make a full contribution to the preparation, performance of the meeting and any follow-up afterwards.

The stages of inspection

A full Inspection process typically comprises three stages of performance (see also Figure 5.1):

- Preparation
- Team Meeting
- Consolidation (or follow-up).

The requirement for Inspections will have been identified in the Project Quality Plan, together with the detailed procedures for conducting them. It is the responsibility of the Moderator to progress and control the Inspection to a satisfactory completion (or of the participants if no Moderator is appointed).

The preparation stage

Preparation can start as much as two working weeks before the date of the meeting, when an Invitation to the Inspection, and a copy of the product for review, is sent by the Moderator to each participant. The Invitation defines the role of the participant, and includes any supporting documentation for

Stages of inspection 73

the product, as relevant to that person's nominated role for the Inspection. For example, if the participant is to be the Peer Reviewer of a design document, then the requirements for that design should be available. If the participant is to assess compliance to standards, a copy of the relevant Standards must be identified and made available.

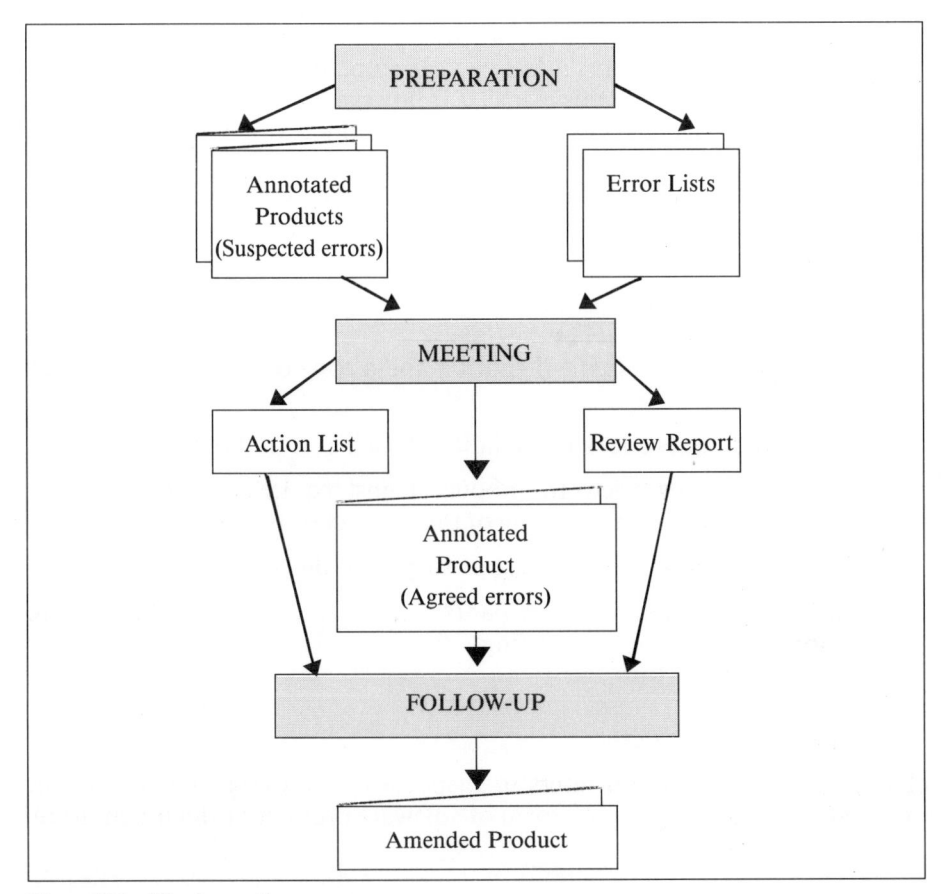

Figure 5.1 The inspection process

Even for relatively informal, low-level Inspections (e.g. of work task products within the phase), this basic process should be followed, and as a minimum, identifying those attending and when and where the meeting will take place, for example, so that independent QA can witness and assess the event.

Each participant must check their availability and competence for their nominated role, and then spend the necessary time to familiarise themselves with the product and generate a list of suspected defects, problems and comments (concentrating on the former). No more than two hours should be needed if the product is of adequate size and complexity for Inspection. (While about half a day of time is needed overall for each participant, this time should be viewed against the time spent developing the product and the likely time saved by detecting defects in the product much earlier than would otherwise be the case.)

Obviously, the more formal the Inspection, the more participants will be needed, and the sooner preparation will need to start, particularly if personnel outside the project or organisation are involved. At any level of formality, it is important that participants make every attempt to prepare and attend, and that management support this priority. If however, someone cannot attend, their list of suspected defects can be passed to the Moderator before the meeting (together with the participant's apologies for absence). The Moderator must decide what action to take, such as postponing the meeting, appointing a substitute or whether someone (even himself) can substitute for the absent participant.

To summarise the organisational aspects of Inspection:

- the Moderator sents the invitation and a copy of the product to each participant;
- the participants check the validity of their role and their availability;
- each participant reviews the product against requirements etc. from their viewpoint and understanding of the product (typically 2 hours spent);
- each participant creates a list of suspected defects and problems;
- if unable to attend, participants send defect list and apologies to Moderator before the meeting.

Performing the inspection

The following description refers to Inspection of a design document; the method can be applied to any form of software product or documentation.

The meeting

The meeting convenes under the chairmanship of the Moderator, who welcomes those participating, outlines the objectives of the meeting, and checks that everyone expected is attending and that they believe themselves competent and prepared for the meeting. (While this should be known beforehand, there is little point in proceeding with the meeting if this check is unsatisfactory; the Moderator should attempt to reconvene the meeting at a later agreed date if possible, or inform the Project Manager of the situation.)

The Designer starts by describing the 'context' of the design e.g. the part of the software requirement addressed by the design, and the overall task the design has to address. The Designer then describes the design step-by-step (or at least those parts of it that are relevant to the Inspection).

The inspection team considers the explanation, and any participant can interrupt either for clarification, or to raise a suspected defect or problem (normally from the list each participant has prepared before the meeting). The meeting, under the control of the Moderator, considers the point raised and attempts to agree whether it is an defect, and/or what further action is needed. Discussion time must be short, to the point, and carefully controlled by the Moderator if the Inspection is going to cover the whole document in the time available.

Inspection criteria

The basis of Inspection (the 'criteria') must be decided before the meeting, so that the appropriate preparation can be done by each participant. Between the participants, a design is inspected against both the design's requirements and any applicable standards; for example, against technical requirements such as interfaces, functional content, execution behaviour, input and output paths and critical design features. These 'terms of reference' or criteria should be derived from the Quality Plan for the project.

Checklists of the points to be covered, or of likely defects in that type of design, are very helpful in achieving maximum efficiency of Inspection.

Recording the outcome

The aim of Inspection is to detect defects in the product and ideally everyone at the meeting agrees whether any defect is there. Usually, there is no need to keep detailed minutes of the meeting, except perhaps where a customer is attending and therefore it is viewed as a formal project meeting. Often, the only record needed from an Inspection is a list (hopefully short!) of defects or defects agreed by the meeting — just as after testing, the main outcome of interest is a list of test failures.

A classification of defects and points arising is very useful for handling the follow-up stage and for demonstrating what the outcome of the Inspection has been (Figure 5.2). A suggested classification is as follows:

— Defect (no solution)
  — defect agreed by the team
  — Author and/or Reviewer actioned to correct defect.
— Defect (with solution)
  — defect and solution agreed by the team
  — product must be modified with the agreed solution and a new version distributed to the Inspection team as evidence.

76 Quality control: Inspection, review and testing

- Action (suggested defect)
  - defect not agreed by the team
  - further investigation needed, and the review repeated.
- Suggestion (Improvement)
  - different approach or solution recommended
  - possible future consideration if relevant.

CLASSIFICATION	STATUS	OUTCOME
Defect (no solution)	Agreed by team	Action to correct defect
Defect (with solution)	Agreed	Modify with agreed solution
Action (suggested defect)	Not Agreed	Investigation re-inspect
Suggestion (improvement)	Accepted	Possible future consideration

Figure 5.2 Recording the outcome of inspection (defect classification)

Part of the skill of the attendees (and the Moderator in particular) is to steer the meeting to concentrate on finding defects within the time available, with the other classes of outcome being looked on as a 'bonus' if included. (Strictly, Fagan Inspection limits the outcome to defects alone, with no consideration of other issues, but it seems unnecessary to waste valuable information about a product if it comes 'free' from the Inspection.)

Handling the defects and follow-up

The results of the meeting are documented immediately (i.e. within a day) by the Moderator, in the form of a written report and record of the outcome of the meeting (this can be a one-page record with defect list attached). A copy is circulated to each participant, and a master copy placed in the project records (Quality File). The report defines any actions on participants (usually the author) to correct defects or to make changes. No other amendments to the inspected item must be made. Strictly, any amendment to the product should require it to be re-inspected, but in practice the meeting will agree if this is necessary (a useful guideline is not to re-inspect any defined changes, provided that the amended product is circulated to participants to check that the change has been made).

The Defect Classification described in Figure 5.2 is helpful in controlling this follow-up.

It is important that follow-up is performed as defined and within a reasonable time (say, one week). If this cannot be achieved, the moderator must report this deficiency to the Project Manager for action. Project management procedures may indicate what extent of rework or timescale is permissible before the Project Manager's agreement is needed; if rework is too extensive, it may upset project progress and damage the project manager's ability to control project progress.

In summary:

- The Moderator documents the meeting results immediately.
- A written report of Inspection and its findings are circulated.
- The Author makes defined changes as actioned.

Design reviews

The Inspection method described above can be adapted to provide a similar basis for Design Reviews (and any other form of project review). A Design Review is a project-level evaluation of project progress involving invited attendees (where relevant, including a customer or user representative). It is based on evaluating one or more deliverables or project-level documents such as a Design Specification, Test Plan or User Document. It is normally a project level meeting and therefore is attended by the Project Manager and possibly more senior management who have a responsibility for the project.

While in practice Design Review meetings often are chaired by the Project Manager, it is preferable that the Chairman has not contributed directly to the project aspects under review; this role corresponds to the Moderator at Inspection. The document(s) concerned may already have been evaluated by means of Inspections of individual parts and/or the entire document.

Checklists

Along with the invitation to review, a checklist of questions relating to the deliverable document(s) and any associated project issues (e.g. has the specification for the document been properly issued) is issued by the Chairman to the invited attendees, e.g:

- Project Manager
- Team Leader

78 Quality control: Inspection, review and testing

- Analyst/Engineer(s) responsible for document
- User representative
- QA representative

This checklist is best as a standard one for this type of document, covering the essential points and any others which experience has shown to be typical (or critical) for this type of document. The questions reflect the criteria being applied (i.e. basis of evaluation) and the objectives of the meeting, e.g. investigating time and cost compliance to the Project Control Plan if it is a Progress Review.

Each attendee answers the checklist questions relevant to his contribution or knowledge of the project, and highlights any which represent possible problems (e.g. an unclear statement in the product specification, or a lack of proper approval for a Test Plan). (Each completed checklist corresponds to the Error List prepared by attendees before Inspection.) Specific sections of questions for specific roles can be useful, to avoid an individual having to assess each question for relevance.

The review meeting can now concentrate on merging the individual checklists into an agreed checklist, and in particular identifying agreed problems or deficiencies (corresponding to the Error List from Inspection). These problems can be classified according to their urgency or criticality to the project e.g:

- agreed problem/defect which prevents acceptance of product and hence progress of project; rework/correction is essential, followed by re-review;
- specific problem/defect with defined solution which can be implemented immediately; limited impact on project/delivery, re-review not necessary;
- unresolved problem/defect; requires further investigation and re-review;
- suggestion or insignificant problem which does not prevent product acceptance or further use; review satisfactory;
- no problem found, review satisfactory.

Any problems found which cannot be expressed by an existing checklist question can be added by an attendee to his checklist, and considered by the review meeting. Questions should be framed such that a negative answer indicates a problem (e.g. 'Have all design requirements been met?'); the meeting can then concentrate on problems indicated by negative answers to checklist questions.

The checklists from review meetings, and corresponding details of problems and follow-up are held in the project's Quality Records (Quality File); this helps to provide evidence that reviews are being held, and that they are making use of project evidence and that the decisions made have this evidence as their basis. The quality of the project is under firm management.

Prevention and improvement

While, understandably, the main initial outcome of Inspections and Reviews is the detection and correction of defects, these events can be used to greater advantage by being used to indicate where improvements in methods and techniques are needed, to prevent the same type of problem occurring again. This changes their emphasis from 'after the event' correction to 'before the event' prevention and improvement. To some extent this happens naturally, since most personnel attending Inspections and Reviews learn lessons from seeing defects in work they have done or have been responsible for, even though review techniques are intended to be impersonal (i.e. 'product not producer'). It is commonly found that the number of defects and problems found by Inspections decreases with time, sometimes substantially. Rather than eliminate Inspections because they no longer appear to be serving a useful purpose (and risk returning to the previous levels of defect), this provides the opportunity to use Inspections and Reviews to build in prevention mechanisms ("how can we stop this happening again?") and to achieve improvement ("how could we have done this better/cheaper/quicker?").

Prevention techniques

One way to prevent problems is to include general prevention techniques in the Inspection criteria. Some examples are:

- *Boundary problems:*
  examine the 'edges' of the specification/design/program/test cases, e.g. what happens when no input or null data is supplied, or when an extreme, but possible, condition applies.

- *Incomplete requirements:*
  ensure that all the 'design inputs' (e.g. functional requirements) have corresponding 'design outputs', i.e. look for incomplete aspects of the product.

- *Misinterpretations and inconsistencies:*
  look for changes in identification of design elements and ensure correct understanding of design inputs (this is one reason for the presentation content of the Inspection process).

- *Incomplete evaluation:*
  look for aspects of the product which are considered vital or important so that their coverage by review is prioritised, for example by the Moderator in the way he handles the progress of the meeting.

A periodic audit of defects not found by Inspection may indicate where change in emphasis is needed. Recording the time taken at review to detect the various classes of defect and their associated cost of correction may indicate how the productivity of Reviews and Inspections can be improved.

Inspections can lead into corrective action on processes and procedures, when it becomes evident that a particular type of defect is recurring. While Inspections are intended to concentrate on finding defects, rather than spending time correcting them, it may be useful once the frequency of defects has fallen to include assessment of the reason for the fault, particularly if it can be identified quickly, with little discussion. Alternatively, the Inspection records can be input to a periodic Improvement Review, where more time is available to assess the origins of defects and to initiate Corrective Action Initiatives. (It should be borne in mind that the BS 5750/ISO 9001 Standard requires a Quality System to include procedures for investigating the cause of 'non-conforming' product and the elimination of potential causes of defect.)

Productivity and defects

The ability of Quality Control processes such as Inspections and Reviews to detect problems early and then correct them relatively quickly and cheaply (before they escalate into more difficult and costly problems), is a very powerful justification for Quality Management practices. Many organisations who introduce Inspection techniques find them very effective, and eventually resulting in increased project productivity, since the 'additional' time and cost spent in the early project stages in handling the extra defects detected more than pays off in reduced testing and maintenance later.

There have been claims that errors may be up to 100 or 200 times more costly to correct in operational systems compared to if they had been corrected initially, e.g. in Specification or Design documents. While it is impossible to verify such claims absolutely (a project is never done twice, with and without Inspections!), if the potential cost of a defect only doubles as it passes to the next development stage, the likely savings are substantial over the typical development life-cycle of five or six sequential phases. By avoiding expensive late corrective work for the smaller cost of Inspections (and some extra time) early in the life cycle, both productivity and quality are improved since fewer defects are left to emerge in the delivered product, and far less support and maintenance is required.

6
Documenting the quality system: The quality manual and quality plans

Introduction

This chapter explains the typical content and structure of an organisations's Quality Manual and associated Project Quality Plans which, together with the Procedures and Standards, document the working Quality System. The BS 5750/ISO 9001 Standard requires the supplier to document his Quality System, including:

- a statement of policy and objectives for quality
- a statement of commitment to quality
- working procedures and instructions.

In practice, every aspect of the Quality System has to be documented to ensure that not only is it fully defined but, importantly, that it can be verified in operation, particularly by an external auditor as part of Assessment to BS 5750/ISO 9001.

While some organisations document their entire Quality System, including Procedures and Standards, in a single volume it is nearly always far more convenient to split it into a number of documents, reflecting the various levels of the Quality System. A large single document may look impressive but, except in the smallest of organisations, is likely to prove impractical to distribute and to keep up-to-date.

The Quality System structure described below is based on the practical experience of organisations, and is also intended to make Quality System Review and Audit tasks much easier. The BS 5750 /ISO 9001 Standard does not specify any particular documentation structure for the Quality System, and therefore an organisation is free to chose whatever structure and grouping of documentation is the most practical.

82 *Documenting and quality system: The quality manual and quality plans*

Organisation of the quality system documentation

The way the documentation is structured needs to take into account a number of factors:

- Stability: as little as possible of the documentation should need re-issue if changes are necessary.
- Localisation: most people want the minimum amount of documentation for the work they do, particularly if they are previously unused to working to documented Procedures.
- Confidentiality: an organisation's working practices will have been built up over a considerable period, and may represent its competitive advantage. While a supplier may be happy to allow some parts of its documented Quality System to be available to a purchaser or client (e.g. as part of a proposal), it may not wish its detailed procedures to be visible externally.

(Note that when a Quality System is formally assessed, the Assessor will need access to any part of the Quality System documentation; however, all information accessed is treated strictly in confidence, and will not be revealed externally.)

The usual way to meet these needs is to document the top-level, organisational aspects of the Quality System (such as statements of Quality Policy and management responsibilities) in a company-level document, usually termed the Quality Manual. It can include related information such as company background and history. This Quality Manual references lower-level, more detailed, documentation such as the Procedure Manuals. Some companies pay much attention to its standard of presentation, even having it typeset and printed on high quality paper – this is because they view the Quality Manual as representing the company's 'shop window' and so is available to customers or other external organisations. Importantly, such a document cannot include confidential company information, which is held in the separate lower-level documents. (Where the Quality System is limited to a part of an organisation, e.g. Group or Division, the Quality Manual originates at the top level of this part, not at the company level.)

Below the level of the Quality Manual is a set of operational documents, including Procedures, Standards and other working practices and information (Figure 6.1). Examples are Procedures Manuals, Operating Instructions and Documentation Standards. As appropriate to their usage, these can be specific to particular work areas and project types, or can be general purpose; it is recommended to group them to match their usage. This level of documentation is sometimes called the Quality Programme; it is available 'on the shelf' for assignment to specific projects or work tasks (with amendment where necessary).

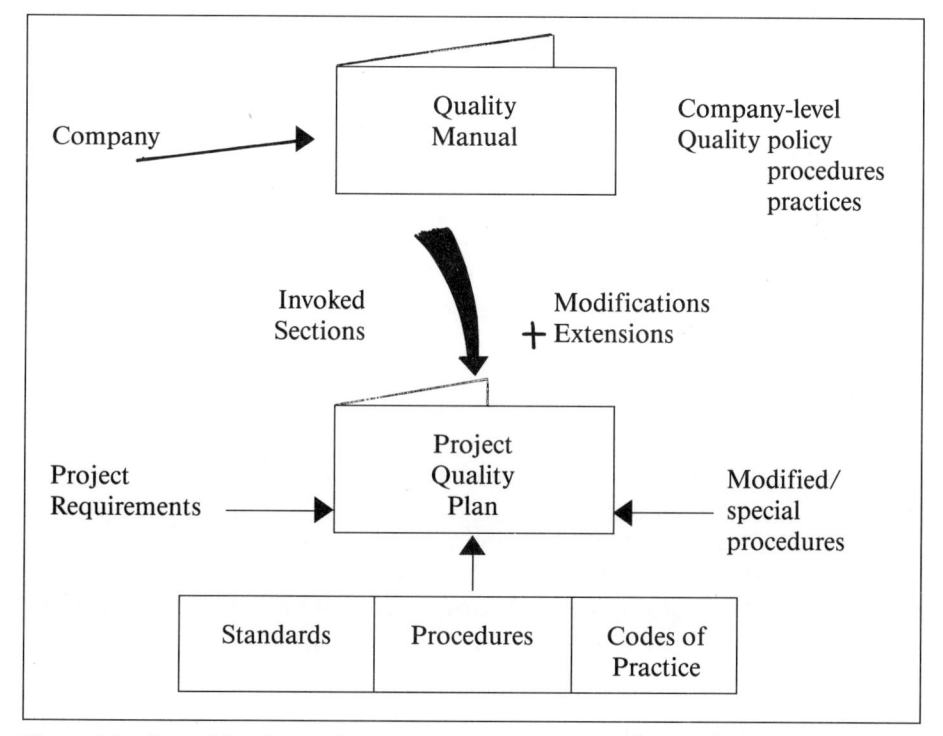

Figure 6.1 Organising the quality systems

At the project level, the various Procedures, Standards and practices defined in the Quality System are assigned to the project by means of references within the Project Quality Plan. While many of these practices should be applicable without change, variations (or even replacements) can be defined in the Quality Plan, provided that they are documented within it or produced as documents referenced from it. All other aspects of the Quality System (e.g. responsibilities, testing practice) relevant to the project must be identified and handled similarly.

The quality manual

What needs to be documented?

As mentioned above, there is no particular format or breakdown of documentation required by BS 5750/ISO 9001, and no two organisations will use exactly the same approach to their Quality System documentation. The following describes a typical structure and content of an organisation's Quality Manual.

84   *Documenting and quality system: The quality manual and quality plans*

Title page

This is the first page of the Manual, and identifies itself as such by stating the official title of the Manual and the organisation to which it applies (including its full name and address). Either on this page or immediately following, the particular copy of the Manual which is being examined should be uniquely identified, so that its issue and circulation is seen to be controlled (as is the case for all Quality System documents). Typically, the master copy is labelled 'master', and other copies are numbered before issue to named recipients. Uncontrolled copies can be generated for circulation to others, provided they are clearly labelled as such, since their update cannot be guaranteed.

Status and control of releases

A Manual is likely to be circulated and updated several times before it is first issued and subsequently may be re-issued when significant company changes occur, such as re-organisation or introduction of new practices. It is best to identify every page of the Manual (and all other Quality System documentation) to show its status and release number (e.g. Draft 3, Issue 2), typically at the bottom right-hand corner. As a minimum, this status must be stated clearly on the title page or immediately after.

Company description

It is useful to include brief details of the company, including its main activities, history and achievements. Also useful is identification of senior personnel such as Chairman, Quality Manager and statement of location(s), particularly if based at several sites. Some companies identify their bankers and solicitors. This information is helpful, both to new employees who are familiarising themselves with the system, and to external purchasers and assessors. The date of BS 5750 Registration (if achieved) is an important milestone to mention at this point.

Preface

As with any document, it is important to allow for easy access and understanding, particularly by those unfamiliar with it. A Preface section contains the following types of information:

- List of Contents
- Record of Amendments
- Statement of Confidentiality
- Statement of Quality Policy
- Distribution and Amendment methods
- Main Section; Description of the Quality System

The quality manual 85

- Any supplementary content relevant to the Manual.

The List of Contents need only identify the sections and content of the Manual, to allow the reader to identify where the information is that he requires. The Record of Amendments is important and it is useful to include the procedure for amending the Manual in an associated section. This Record ensures that the Manual can be checked as being up-to-date, that all amendments have been made (and by whom) and dated. A single page list should suffice; if the number of amendments cannot be fitted on the page, than the Manual is probably ready for re-issue, since the likelihood of at least one holder not having a fully up-to-date Manual will be increasing. The list identifies:

- amendment number/date of issue
- page(s) affected
- brief details
- initials of person inserting the amendment
- the date it was done.

The Statement of Quality Policy is a vital requirement of a BS 5750/ISO 9001 Quality System. It can be brief (a couple of sentences), but sets the background for the direction and emphasis of the Quality System. It should be stated clearly and given the highest authority possible (e.g. signed by the Managing Director or Chairman). As an example:

> " The Quality Policy of Software Systems Ltd is to supply our customers with products and services which are designed, developed and implemented to high professional standards, and intended to meet fully the customer's needs. We aim to satisfy our customers at all stages of design and development and in all aspects of our products and services.
>
> To support this policy, Software Systems Ltd operates a comprehensive Quality System which applies to all work undertaken for our customers. All techniques, methods, procedures and standards are managed and controlled within this System. Software Systems Ltd are committed to its continual maintenance and improvement."

The statement of Quality Policy can be displayed on notice boards and elsewhere around the company (e.g. reception), and circulated to staff to ensure they are aware of it and understand its significance. It must be included in the Quality Manual.

86 *Documenting and quality system: The quality manual and quality plans*

Distribution and amendment methods

As explained in more detail in an earlier chapter, every copy of the Quality Manual must be positively identified, for example by a serial number (with the master copy clearly identified as such) as this meets one of the requirements for Document Control. The Quality Manager (or other nominated person) controls distribution and maintains a record of who has been issued with copies (and the individual number). A signature of the holder can be obtained to record receipt.

Amendment methods must be clearly defined and adhered to. Typically, the Quality Manager is responsible for the issue and distribution of amendments, and the copy holder is responsible for their incorporation. These responsibilities (or equivalents) need to be stated in the Quality Manual. It is recommended to apply the same identification methods (e.g. issue/version numbering) as for other Quality System documentation.

The main section

One of the decisions to be made is whether the structure of the main section of the Manual reflects the twenty paragraphs of BS 5750 Part 1/ISO 9001 in order to make it easy for assessment or whether to structure it to reflect company needs. The latter is recommended for two main reasons:

- BS 5750 is not structured particularly conveniently for software development work (the ISO 9000-3 interpretation is considerably different);
- by far the most common use of the Manual will be by the company itself, not by an external BS 5750 assessor.

It is useful to include a cross-reference table to BS 5750/ISO 9001 as guidance for assessment purposes, and to give confidence internally that all its requirements have been addressed by the Quality System.

A sample content of the main section of the manual is described below:

- **Terms and Definitions relating to Quality.**
  It is useful to provide a set of definitions of quality terms (e.g. Quality Control, Quality Assurance) to ensure that everyone reading the Manual has a common understanding of basic terminology. (BS 4778 is a useful source of reference.)

- **Company Organisation, usually including an organisational chart.**
  This describes the structure of the company, including specific responsibilities for quality, from Board level down. The Quality Manager role (or equivalent) must be included, with a statement of access to the top level of the company. Responsibilities for Quality

Assurance (e.g. a QA department) and Quality Control (e.g. Project and Line Managers) should be included.

- **Summary and description of Quality System content and operation.**
  This describes the scope of the System, identifying to which types of work and organisational areas it applies (e.g. all development projects for external customers, proposals for such work, and supporting services and facilities). Quality Management and technical practice on the work within its scope is summarised, for example, identifying that a Project Manager is appointed to control each project.

  (Other useful information at this point is a general Quality Strategy, e.g. stating that all work is organised as projects and requires a Quality Plan to be raised by the Project Manager and approved by the appropriate Line Manager. The roles of independent QA personnel in project work and in supporting the Quality System can be summarised.)

- **Summary and breakdown of Quality System Documentation structure.**
  All Quality System documentation must be capable of being referenced back to this section, so it identifies what types and grouping exist (procedures, standards, mandatory, guidance, etc.). In a small or straightforward Quality System, this section can include a Documentation Index, but it is better to reference groups of documents to avoid frequent changes to this section. For software work, it is helpful to group the technical documentation around a life-cycle model.

- **Description of Quality System Review and Audit process.**
  It can be useful to highlight these aspects of the Quality System, particularly if Certification to BS 5750 is an objective. It will explain these processes and their significance.

(Where a standard life-cycle model or development approach is used for most or all work, it can be described at this level of the Manual; otherwise this information will be included at the project level.)

A checklist for quality manual content

The following list represents typical contents of the main section of a Quality Manual:

- Statement of scope of Quality System (organisational areas, products, projects, support functions, etc.).
- Definition, structure and relationship of Quality Control, Quality Assurance and Quality Management activities.
- How quality is built in and controlled within the work activities (e.g. by Quality Plans).

88 *Documenting and quality system: The quality manual and quality plans*

- Responsibilities within the Quality Management System.
- Description of roles, responsibilities and tasks for Quality Control, Quality Assurance and Quality Management activities.
- Identification and/or Overview of the set of Quality System documentation.
- Clarification of status of documentation (mandatory/optional/guidance).

Quality plans

While the Quality Manual, Procedures and Standards Manuals and similar documents define how the Quality System works, and the work practices that are available for project work, lower level documentation will provide a precise definition of the quality-related requirements for project work. This is provided by means of a Project Quality Plan (or equivalent); preferably it is a separate document from the normal Project Plan defined by the Project Manager for monitoring and control purposes, for several reasons:

- it is the clearest way of demonstrating that project quality requirements are defined and provided for;
- it should require less frequency and extent of modification than the Project Plan, since the latter is time and resource-dependent and therefore more likely to change during a project;
- it makes it easier to review the audit project quality practice; e.g. do the project quality records correspond directly to those called for in the Project Quality Plan?

If existing project practice makes it inconvenient to create a separate Project Quality Plan, then ensure that the parts of the Project Plan which correspond to it are clearly identified.

The contents of a project quality plan

The following information is recommended for inclusion in a Project Quality Plan. Note that where the information exists in other documents (e.g. where existing procedures are to be used on the project or a separate Test Plan is created), a precise reference to the document is an acceptable substitute – indeed this can be preferred since it helps to avoid any inadvertent misinterpretation of duplicated or summarised information in the Plans.

Where a variation on the usual procedure is required, this variation (and preferably the reason for it) is defined and referenced to the procedure at this point. If the variations to a procedure are extensive, it can be better to include a complete re-definition of the procedure for this project within the Quality Plan.

An individual Project Quality Plan may range in size from a few pages, where the Project is small or straightforward (and therefore its content is mostly references to other standard Quality System documents), to a document of considerable size and detail for a large or complex project where much of the Quality Plan content has to be developed specially. However, one of the benefits of an established Quality System should be that comparatively little work is needed to define an individual Quality Plan for projects of a similar nature.

Suggested quality plan headings

The following headings are suggested for a Project Quality Plan intended to meet the requirements of a BS 5750/ISO 9001 Quality System. Individual headings can be combined or altered as project circumstances require, although it is useful to retain a consistent set across similar projects to assist comparison and to help ensure that all Quality Plan requirements have been met (see also Figure 6.2).

```
Purpose
Project Description
Quality Plan Management and Implementation
References
Documentation
Standards, Procedures and Working Practices
Evaluation
Configuration Management
Software Control
Problem Reporting and Corrective Action
Methods, Tools and Techniques
Supplier Control
Quality Records
Test Management
Progress Monitoring and Reporting
Maintenance
Supplier and Purchaser Activities
```

Figure 6.2 Quality plan headings

Purpose

The Quality Plan, like every document within the Quality System, should be self-defining, stating its purpose, its scope of applicability (e.g. to which Project(s) it applies), and its relationship with other documents. Headings under this section can include:

- objectives and scope;
- identification and brief definition of project(s) to which it applies;
- relationship to other project and Quality System documents (in particular the Project Plan, Purchaser or Contract Documents, internal and external requirements for Standards and Procedures, etc.).

Project description

This section describes and summarises the project (in particular the Life-cycle Model to be applied and/or the project structure and organisation). This description is sufficiently detailed that it is clear how the contents of this Plan can be applied to the project. Project deliverables and intermediate Stage products should be identified and summarised. Detailed, comprehensive project information can be provided in other forms of Project Plan such as Management, Technical, Testing and Delivery Plans, as long as they are clearly referenced from the Quality Plan (see below).

For a larger project, it may be more convenient to draw up initially a project level Quality Plan, followed later by more detailed Stage Quality Plans for individual stages. The Project Quality Plan defines project-wide quality activities and summarises stage-based activities.

The management, technical and quality organisation of the project should be summarised, including any user, customer or contractual content (management of the Quality Plan is included in a corresponding section below) and should include:

- identification and summary of project(s) to which the plan applies;
- life-cycle model and project stages;
- list and description of project deliverables and stage products;
- project organisation.

Methods, tools and techniques to be applied to the project work (i.e. how the work is to be done) are defined in a separate section below, but alternatively could be included in this section.

Quality plan management and implementation

It is important to define exactly how the plan is to be managed, particularly if changes are anticipated during the course of the project. Responsibilities for the plan's generation, authorisation, compliance and review are stated to demonstrate that there is control of quality throughout the project. Usually, generation and operation of the plan are responsibilities of the Project Manager, although Quality personnel can advise and assist if requested. The plan is reviewed and authorised by senior personnel with the appropriate Management, Technical and Quality responsibilities (e.g. Development Manager, Senior Engineer/Analyst, Quality Manager).

Increasingly, customers and users are requiring participation in project quality activities (e.g. project review); such representatives should be identified in the Quality Plan, and the agreed level and extent of their participation stated.

This section also describes how the plan will be managed within the project, e.g. project team responsibilities for Quality Control, such as:

- review and authorisation of the Plan;
- maintenance and update;
- responsibilities for implementation (internal and external);
- project organisation and reporting for quality (including independent QA);
- identification of project personnel and their skills/qualifications.

Another aspect of Quality Plan Management to clarify at this point is the level of quality management required by the project; for instance, a project to upgrade application software to be used internally will not require the same level and extent of quality management as the development of new software for an external customer or for live operation in a user department.

References

This section provides a definitive list of documents (including their issue or version) referenced from all parts of the plan; it is likely to include:

- Quality System documents (including the Quality Manual);
- other Project Plans (Management, Technical, etc.);
- specifications, standards, etc. applicable to the project, e.g. Standards and Procedures Manuals;
- customer or contractual documents applicable to the project.

This section of the Plan should be looked on as the formal 'attachment' of these documents to the project, even though they may be mentioned in other project documents (e.g. Purchaser Requirements). It is recommended that it is indicated whether any variation to the documented procedures etc. is required for the Project (to be defined in Standards, Practices and Conventions below).

(This References section is sometimes provided as an Appendix to the Quality Plan.)

92 *Documenting and quality system: The quality manual and quality plans*

Documentation

This section defines how Project Documentation (both internally generated and external in origin) will be handled. It is useful to maintain a project document list of all such identified documents. Procedures for their production, review and control should be defined or referenced. Content includes:

- document list;
- document identification, review and control procedures.

[handwritten annotation: *In progress - at top of every sub & at least every screen full if long sub.]

Standards, procedures and working practices

This section identifies the Standards, Procedures and other definitions of Working Practices which are to be applied to the project; normally, the documents they are contained in are those referenced above. This section includes any variations on normal practices such as revised procedures adopted for the project, preferably with an explanation of why the variation is necessary. (By documenting them here, authorisation of these variations is covered by overall authorisation of the Quality Plan.)

It is useful to clarify which documentation represents mandatory practice, and which is not (e.g. Codes of Practice, Programming Guides).

Evaluation

Having stated the project quality practice in the relevant section above, the means of monitoring compliance to the Plan is defined here. This includes techniques such as Audits, Reviews, Inspections and Walkthroughs, covering the Quality Assurance and Quality Control requirements of the project. The Procedures and Standards for the performance of these techniques can be included above, with this section indicating when and how they are to be applied, e.g. which type of activities require Inspection and how participants will be selected. The schedule of evaluation events (i.e. specific dates), and other detail can be stated in the Project Control Plan if more convenient (but make this clear in this section of the Quality Plan). If this information is provided in both Plans, ensure that it is consistent.

Any methodology or approach to quality evaluation, e.g. the basis for selecting project activities for Audit should be identified. The independent element of quality practices should be evident, such as the use of peer review or the involvement of personnel acting in an independent QA role.

(Note that while Testing can be considered to be a form of Quality Control, it is often more convenient to define it in a separate Project Test Plan.)

Configuration management (product control)

This section defines how the various project components and products (both software and documentation) are identified and controlled. In larger projects this may be a separate Configuration Management Plan. Topics covered include:

- identification of configuration items (i.e. which project components and products will be controlled);
- control and reporting of the status of items (e.g. whether tested, authorised for delivery, etc.);
- control of change, including reporting and assessment of defects or improvements and tracking their implementation;
- interrelationship of software items and their documentation;
- handling of external items (e.g. utility software, customer documents);
- operation of (and responsibility for) a Project Library to retain custody of master items and to control their duplication and issue.

Configuration Management should result in all project items being identified and their evolution through the project being controlled and traceable, for example, it should be possible to track a design module through coding, to when it is built into the complete software. Also, to identify corresponding documentation and whether it was changed at the same time as the module. Configuration Management tracks the approval and authorisation status of the items. Only appropriately authorised items should be used by a project or delivered by it.

Software control (code, documentation and media)

Depending on the extent of this requirement within the project, this may be a specific section of the plan or part of the Configuration Management section above. It defines the methods and facilities needed for physical custody of the project items, both software and documentation, and particularly for deliverable items. It is closely related to the Project Library requirement in the section above. Topics include:

- storage and custody of software items (i.e. executable code, both deliverable and internal);
- storage and custody of documentation (in particular master copies);
- security of physical media (e.g. disks used to store and deliver software items).

Problem reporting and corrective action

The BS 5750/ISO 9001 Standard mentions this aspect of Quality Management practice specifically. The Quality Plan should indicate how problems and defects found during the project (particularly as a result of Quality Control and Assurance activities) will be handled. This requirement also covers problems found in the methods and processes used by the project (procedures, methods and techniques, etc.). Topics to be covered include:

- reporting, assessing and resolving problems and defects;
- defining and progressing corrections;
- responsibilities.

It is useful to show how any conflicts of project time and cost are resolved against the need to make corrections (e.g. by some form of Defect Control or Change Assessment review method).

These procedures work closely with Configuration Management processes identified above.

Methods, tools, and techniques

The plans for a project must define how the product is to be created; that is, the methods, tools and techniques to be used. This section defines this information, or provides references to where the information can be found, e.g. in a separate Project Technical Plan. This section may reference external documents, e.g. *SSADM Manual*, when externally defined methods are being used. The actual usage of methods, particularly variations or partial usage, should be clear, typically by reference to the relevant internal procedures:

- project-wide methods (e.g. project management, quality assurance);
- life-cycle stage methods (e.g. analysis and design and other technical stages);
- relationship to external methods and extent of usage of these methods;
- technical, management, quality and support activities.

Supplier control

Any product or service supplied from outside the project should have its quality and effectiveness evaluated to a level and extent reflecting its importance to the project. As a minimum, the performance of the supplier (internal or external) should be recorded; if the product is to be used by the project (e.g. software package), then a suitable level of verification of the product (reflecting its usage on the project) and on the organisation supplying it (e.g. extent of support availabale) should be made before it is obtained. Such a record should include:

- assurance of supplier products;
- assurance of sub-contracted work and components;
- relationship to other internal departments or personnel and appropriate controls;
- monitoring and recording of supplier performance.

N/a

It is becoming more common to handle the relationship between service providers by some form of Service Level Agreement, which includes actions to be taken if the supplier service does not meet its requirements.

Quality records

This section is important, since it covers the establishment and retention of all the records needed to analyse and demonstrate the effectiveness of the project. One useful practice is to set up Quality, Technical and Management Files for the project records (held on computer or as documentation, as preferred). For large projects, these files may themselves represent groups of records. The records should include the following:

- list of records to be created and their organisation;
- handling of records: identification, filing and custody, storage, maintenance;
- period of retention;
- customer or client access.

Test management

It is likely that a separate Project Test Plan is created for the project (or within the Technical Plan), in which case this section will reference that particular plan, with possibly a summary of its content and approach included in this section; otherwise, the Quality Plan will include the following information:

- test requirements;
- test strategy and management;
- responsibilities and personnel involvement (including QA, customer/users);
- test specifications and criteria;

- test methods, equipment and environment;
- test plans and procedures for performing the tests;
- test records and authorisation;
- acceptance tests.

Progress monitoring and reporting

While most of this information will usually be defined in a separate Project Control Plan, it is useful to summarise it here (e.g. the project management methodology and use of supporting tools) and to indicate how much of this information will be accessed for Quality Management purposes:

- project management organisation and responsibilities;
- customer/user involvement;
- progress review practice and participation;
- project schedule, costs and resources.

Maintenance

Even for a purely development project, this section may be required, either where the ability to maintain the product is part of the customer requirements or where some of the product is delivered early, for example for trial or assessment purposes. Other possible aspects of maintenance where documentation needs to be updated is to reflect software changes and/or where the customer wishes to participate in the maintenance activities. It will define the maintenance process, often with reference to the closely related tasks of Configuration Management and Change Control.

In addition, responsibilities for maintenance must be stated.

Supplier and purchaser activities

In some projects, the purchasing organisation may require to monitor the project while it progresses (e.g. at end-stage reviews, or by regular project reviews) as part of their approach to Quality Management. While these aspects of project work can be covered in the various sections of the Quality Plan, it can be useful to collect or summarise them within a particular section of the plan. The activities are:

- Supplier responsibilities to the purchaser (e.g. provision of project information and access to personnel).

- Purchaser involvement and responsibility (e.g. attendance at project reviews, provision of test-related information).
- Problem handling and corrective action mechanisms.

Summary

The headings described above are meant to be representative of the contents of a complete Quality Plan for a development project; they can be adapted to meet the circumstances and scale of any individual project. Other types of project (or ongoing work e.g. maintenance) should operate under a comparable Quality Plan, such that all work done, tests performed, information provided and responsibilities exercised are defined (or referenced) in the Quality Plan.

It will take some time to set up a working Quality Plan where none has been done before, but by taking care to define it so it can be adapted to other related work, it becomes a very effective means of managing quality; it defines for both internal and external purposes what is to be achieved, how it is done and how the outcome can be evaluated.

Writing and authorising the project quality plan

The Project Quality Plan is best written by the Project Manager, with contributions where necessary from others with specific skills or responsibilities for the project (team leader, senior analyst, designer, etc.). Aspects which are quality-specific (e.g. QA techniques) can be written by QA staff if required specifically for the project. The most important requirement is that it is acceptable to project personnel and therefore workable.

The Plan needs to be agreed and approved, typically by line management (or equivalent) to whom the Project Manager is responsible and (for the quality-related aspects) by the Quality Manager. Where the project is the result of a contract with a purchaser, it is becoming more common for the purchaser to require to formally review and accept it before finalising the contract – in effect treating it as the first project deliverable. In this case, the Quality Plan will exist at two levels, the top (project) level being the subject of purchaser agreement, and the lower, detailed, (Stage) level remaining an internal document for the developer.

7
Introducing a quality system

Introduction

The number of organisations who develop software or IT systems and who have a Certified BS 5750/ISO 9001 Quality System is still small, but considerably more are interested in the benefits of doing this or are finding that evidence of Quality Management practice is being requested by an increasing number of their purchasers (some expect the majority of software developers will introduce some form of Quality System over the next few years). Organisations who have introduced a Quality System have found it to be a feasible and worthwhile exercise, and one which offers considerable internal and external benefits.

In the UK, the Department of Trade and Industry (DTI) has for several years been encouraging industry to improve its efficiency and competitiveness – one important way is to introduce a Quality System. For example, its Quality Initiative has offered subsidised consultancy to smaller companies to help them to introduce a Quality System, and there are a number of other schemes which encourage companies to adopt Quality Improvement and Total Quality Management programmes.

Introducing a Quality System is a major task – for most organisations it takes around 18 months and requires between one and two man-years of effort. Its impact on working practice can be considerable, and so it is important to plan, implement and monitor the introduction carefully.

What is involved?

The most important message is: treat it like a project. This means as a minimum:

- obtain senior management commitment and authorisation for the project (via some form of Project Initiation process);

- appoint a project manager (usually the prospective Quality Manager) and a Steering Committee which includes senior management and 'user' representation;
- produce and agree a Project Plan (which identifies the project stages) and which is approved by the Steering Committee;
- monitor and control the introduction of the Quality System against the plan (with a regular review and decision-making process);
- close down the introduction project when the defined objective has been reached (usually successful assessment against BS 5750); the task then changes to maintenance and improvement of the System (potentially a continuous programme).

The introduction as a project

Introducing a Quality System is a complex process, for a variety of reasons:

- it is only done once by an organisation;
- there is both tangible and intangible content (e.g. production of documentation, staff awareness training);
- it has to take place alongside the organisation's normal business – only exceptionally can this be disrupted;
- by definition, everyone who will work within the Quality System will be affected – personnel and 'user' aspects need to be considered carefully;
- other internal departments, external customers and suppliers will all be affected to some degree;
- both considerable time and cost are involved.

Another benefit of handling the Introduction as a project is that it gives a foretaste of what 'normal life' will be like once the Quality System is operating – if management of the introduction is troublesome, then this may give an early warning of possible problems in Quality System operation.

The stages of introduction

A Quality System needs to be introduced in stages, with each stage finishing at a 'breakpoint' or 'milestone', where progress can be assessed against tangible targets (e.g. have all Procedures been completed and introduced?). At the end of each stage, the project is thoroughly reviewed with senior management and the Steering Committee to verify achievement of the project plan and to sanction progression to the next stage. Modifications to the overall plan and/or to the next stage plans may be necessary. This may reflect, for example, better understanding of what is involved, or changed organisational circumstances such as different priorities for resources or a more urgent timescale to introduce the Quality System.

The set of stages described below is based on the experience of organisations who have introduced a Quality System. Stage 4 (Assessment) is not relevant if certification against BS 5750/ISO 9001 is not an objective; however most organisations find that Certification provides a very tangible measure of achievement. Stage 5 follows from successful introduction (and so, strictly speaking, lies beyond the introduction project).

   Stage 1 : Preparation and Planning
   Stage 2 : Introduction
   Stage 3 : Operation (Run the Quality System)
   Stage 4 : Assessment
   Stage 5 : Improvement

As with any project, the ideal of carefully separated stages may be difficult to achieve in practice; however, the closer it is achieved in reality, the more manageable the project will be.

The need for separate stages

When introducing a Quality System, there are some considerations to be balanced against the need for clear-cut stages:

- the need to achieve and demonstrate benefits as early as possible; for example, by introducing the system in some areas before others, rather than across all areas at the same time;

- uncertainty as to how much work is involved; for example, by piloting the introduction of some sample Procedures;

- requirements of particular customers for Quality System introduction in a timescale too short for full introduction across the organisation;

- difficulties of introducing the Quality System on existing projects;

- impending reorganisation within the company.

It is recommended to put together a strategy for introducing the Quality System which recognises and balances these factors (e.g. which operational areas first, how to bring existing work into the System).

Another factor to be considered is to what extent the Quality System introduction needs to include Quality Improvement. If some areas of practice (e.g. Contract Review, or Inspection and Test) do not meet the requirements of BS 5750 ISO 9001, they must be improved accordingly if Certification is an objective. Quality System introduction is an obvious opportunity to improve basic quality practice. In general, substantial changes in practice should be postponed until the Quality System has been introduced, to avoid compromising the main purpose of the project.

The end of Stage 1 will be the review and agreement of the overall project plan for Quality System introduction, with a firm commitment from senior management to proceed. (Detailed stage plans can be produced at the start of the relevant stage.)

Stage 1: preparation and planning

One of the first tasks is to obtain a firm commitment from Senior Management to introducing the Quality System (e.g. as a 'public' statement to all staff). The stage can then proceed under the guidance of the Project Manager (Quality Manager). Once this has been done, a number of 'scene-setting' tasks are appropriate:

- Circulate the news to staff that the commitment has been made and arrange a series of short meetings with staff to answer questions and to gauge support. Make it clear that the Quality System will be a permanent feature of company practice.

- Decide the scope and objectives of the Quality Sytsem, including the areas to which it will apply (particularly if being introduced in certain areas first).

- Produce a Quality Policy statement and draft Quality Manual; if few or any procedures exist, produce some sample ones for illustration.

- Produce an outline plan for the introduction, in particular to demonstrate the feasible time and cost.

- Consider implementing a 'pilot scheme' on a project or area if there is still significant doubt or lack of understanding.

- Arrange training sessions and staff briefings to introduce specific techniques and aspects of Quality System practice (e.g. performing Inspections, procedure-writing, etc.).

It may be useful at this point to obtain information from other sources who have a Quality System such as similar organisations or from external consultants. External sources can provide very useful guidance and support; however, it is important that the Quality System which is created is fully suited to its organisation's particular needs.

It can be helpful to indentify a 'champion' for the project, who will 'endorse' and support the project, and who has the support of both staff and management. A long serving, respected, middle manager may be suitable.

Completing the stage

The end of this stage should be marked by a Progress Review, at which achievement is assessed and a detailed project plan for the next stage (Introduction) is approved. The tangible product is the draft Quality Manual, incorporating the Quality Policy Statement. Points to be confirmed include:

- Are the objectives of introducing the Quality System fully defined, agreed and believed to be achievable?
- Is its scope fully identified and agreed?
- Have staff in all areas affected been contacted and is their attitude favourable?
- What are the outcome and associated benefits (internal and external) expected to be?
- What is the expected cost and timescale, and is it acceptable?
- Are outside resources or advice needed?

Changing methods and practices

Introduction of a Quality System requires effective, but stable, practices. There will need to be a balance between *necessary* changes to methods and practices to make them adequate for the System and *preferred* changes which, while desirable, may cause delay or disruption to the introduction of the system. For development work, a complete life-cycle model, including technical, management and quality practices, provides the best 'foundation' for the set of Quality System methods and practices. It is worth making any necessary changes to the life-cycle before the Quality System is introduced. Similarly, any changes needed in other areas (e.g. supplier control) are best implemented ahead of the Quality System.

Stage 2: introduction

This stage will incur most of the costs and require the closest management attention; it is likely to need the full-time involvement of the Project Manager. Regular review (no longer than monthly) is essential, since most problems can be expected in this stage.

104 *Introducing a quality system*

The first step is to produce detailed project plans. A project planning tool capable of producing bar-charts, recording resources and costs and representing progress is very useful (such tools may already be used for planning projects).

Questions to be addressed include:

- To what extent is introduction vertical or horizontal (i.e. uniformly across all areas and projects or completely into specific areas or projects first)?
- Will staff need awareness, education and training? (This may vary from area to area and, from person to person; and it must precede changes in working or the need for new skills.)
- Are staff available to define and write their own Procedures and standards? (While it is important that staff make a significant contribution, project and work pressures may limit this possibility – in which case external help will be needed.)
- What is the best timing for bringing individual areas and projects within the Quality System? (E.g. it will not make sense to disrupt projects nearing completion or areas already undergoing change.)
- Is there adequate time contingency? (Project and organisational priorities will often override Quality System introduction – this can delay progress significantly. Allow as much as one month in every two elapsed months.)
- Is there adequate cost contingency? (It should be possible to identify the work tasks and cost them reasonably accurately, but like 'real' projects, most organisations find costs are greater than they initially expected – allow for 20% contingency or more.)
- What resources and costs are included? (Strictly, all costs incurred, e.g. Procedure writing, Inspections, etc. should be attributed to the Quality System introduction – but cost benefits will be realised in operational areas by new and improved working practices.)

(It may be more relevant to cost one-off costs, e.g. training, against Quality System introduction, but view 'running' costs such as holding Inspections as operational or project costs.)

Stage 3: operation

Once the Quality System has been introduced, it must be operated for sufficient time to detect and correct any problems and to confirm that it is operating properly. This is especially important if it is to be assessed against BS 5750/ISO 9001, otherwise Certification will not be achieved.

A most important task is to perform regular internal Quality Audit on the Quality System. On an established Quality System, this is done typically over a period of 12 months, but for a new Quality System it should be more frequent and comprehensive. The Quality Manager should aim to audit the entire Quality System, both to ensure that it is working completely and to firmly establish the Quality Audit process. Corrective action to address problems and defects must be performed and followed-up rigorously – this is a common reason for non-compliances being found when a new Quality System is externally assessed.

In practice, a period of at least six months is recommended for operating and stabilising the Quality System, to the point where it is suitable for assessment.

Operations stage checklist

- Ensure customers and suppliers know you are introducing a Quality System (particularly those who have expressed interest or requested its introduction), and remind them how it will affect the way you work with them. Emphasise that you need to adhere to it strictly once it is operating.

- Resist avoidable changes to the Quality System before it is assessed – the Quality System needs to be as stable as possible. Wherever possible, delay such changes until Stage 5 (Improvement).

- Ensure that all projects, operations and areas within the scope of the Quality System are brought into it and are operating to its requirements. (There may still be some projects coming to completion which are allowed to remain outside the Quality System.)

- Arrange regular feedback sessions with staff, and be receptive to *ad-hoc* comment which indicates whether the Quality System is being accepted – look particularly for weak points. Also listen to project and operational managers and those who have responsibilities within the system. (This feedback must be clearly separate from formal Quality System Audit.)

- Start to establish (and quantify if possible) the benefits achieved, and identify where working practice has changed – this is easier if this was anticipated at the Planning Stage. (A survey of management and staff reaction may be useful.)

At the end of the Operation Stage, the Quality System will be ready for formal assessment. There will usually be overlap with this next Stage, since preparatory contact with the Certification Body and the assessor will be necessary prior to the intended assessment date.

106   *Introducing a quality system*

Stage 4: assessment

While this stage is the shortest in terms of time and cost, it requires careful preparation – and if the prime objective of introducing the Quality System is to obtain Certification against BS 5750/ISO 9001, then it is the key stage. (Note, however, that most organisations find that the internal benefits achieved by a Quality System by the time it is operating more than justify its introduction.)

It is recommended to contact the assessing organisation (Certification Body) several months before the target assessment date. Indeed, there is no harm in initial contact being made at the Introduction Stage to confirm what is involved and the likely cost. An assessor will be in contact to ensure that assessment is worthwhile, to explain the process and to answer queries. (Most companies find this contact very useful.)

There are currently a comparatively limited number of organisations capable of performing assessments against BS 5750/ISO 9001 for IT development work (see Appendix A). Most currently certified software and IT suppliers have used the British Standards Institution for assessment, but there are others. However, the Department of Trade and Industry is currently establishing a formal assessment scheme for the IT sector (the TickIT Project), which is intended to result in a wider choice of assessing organisations and more availability of assessors with experience of software and IT work. This will also make it easier to obtain competitive quotations; the cost of a typical assessment can be considerable, depending on the size of the assessed company, the variety of work performed and the complexity of the Quality System.

It is strongly recommended that a dummy Quality System audit is performed about one month before the formal audit. As well as identifying non-compliances which would prevent successful assessment (and allowing time for correction), it ensures that everyone knows what is involved, how the audit process works and what the outcome is likely to be. It is also useful for the dummy audit to be more extensive than the later formal audit, to ensure that everyone is fully prepared, even though not all aspects of the Quality System may be examined at the formal audit.

Assessment stage checklist

- Select the assessment organisation (Certification Body) sufficiently in advance (at least three months before, preferably as soon as the Quality System documentation is complete).
- Act on advice provided by the assessment organisation.
- Perform a dummy audit before the formal assessment and act on the findings immediately.

- Ensure everyone knows and understands the purpose of assessment, and is available and prepared on the day.
- Help the assessor by providing the facilities requested and full access to personnel and documentation.
- Accept any non-compliances found at assessment, perform corrective action within the agreed timescale and ensure the evidence of effectiveness of the action is obtained.
- Once certification has been achieved, review the outcome with senior management, agree any remaining changes and the point at which the introduction project is wound-up (to be replaced by improvement and maintenance of the Quality System).
- Inform purchasers, suppliers and internal staff of successful Certification (Registration).

Note that it is not unusual for a first assessment to reveal non-compliances against either the organisation's own Quality System or against the BS 5750 Standard. Once they are corrected, and evidence provided to the assessor, Certification is granted – with a typical delay of one to three months. Even if the number or the significance of non-compliances means that a complete re-assessment is required, it makes little sense not to take the necessary action considering the time and effort already spent to get this far through Quality System introduction.

Stage 5: improvement

Once the Quality System has been assessed and certification granted, operation should be allowed to settle down before making any improvements identified during the Operation and Assessment stages. Note, however, that a reasonable level of Quality System improvement and maintenance is a requirement of BS 5750.

Improvement stage checklist

- Make desirable improvements which strengthen the achievements of the Quality System (e.g. improve training programmes, clarify procedures, tighten quality controls). These improvements may have been identified at the Operation Stage, but not yet implemented.
- Monitor achievement of internal benefits and the reaction of external suppliers and customers.

108 *Introducing a quality system*

- Identify further objectives which could be achieved by the Quality System (e.g. a costs of quality programme, or Quality Improvement initiative).
- Remember to expect surveillance visits by the Certification Body — they are likely to be more frequent or rigorous for a recent Quality System, or if non-compliances have been found in previous audits.
- Use internal Quality System Audit to take an overall view of the Quality System and its effectiveness as well as to identify problems.
- Continue to obtain *ad-hoc* and informal feedback from staff at all levels.

It is often possible to simplify procedures and methods of working with experience of Quality System operation. An over-elaborate Quality System is to no-one's advantage.

Some organisations find that the emphasis of quality control changes once a Quality System is established, from being primarily an error-detection process, towards being able to analyse why problems occur and to make corresponding improvements in working practice, i.e. it becomes more of a Quality Improvement process. Beyond this, the Quality System provides a platform from which to start Total Quality Management initiatives.

8
Quality improvement and total quality

Introduction

A BS 5750/ISO 9001 Quality System does not have to be an end in itself; it can be seen as the platform from which to launch further into programmes of Quality Improvement and Total Quality Management. As stated in the previous chapter, the BS 5750/ISO 9001 Standard includes requirements for corrective action to Quality System processes and for their improvement. These requirements are both reactive and pre-emptive:

- investigating the causes of 'non-conforming' product and perfoming corrective actions to prevent the same problem recurring (*reactive*);
- analysing information about the products and work processes to detect and eliminate potential causes of non-conformance (*pre-emptive*).

BS 5750/ISO 9001 requires procedures for these types of corrective action. Other improvement-related requirements of the Standard include:

- action to prevent product non-conformity;
- updating of quality control techniques when necessary;
- regular review of the effectiveness of the Quality System (usually achieved by regular Quality System audit).

Changes and improvements to the Quality System can be made as the need arises. However, while improvement is not a strong feature of the BS 5750/ISO 9001 requirements, it does not prevent Quality Improvement initiatives being carried out in addition to any arising from normal Quality System operation.

Quality improvement and quality systems

A Quality Improvement initiative can include two basic types of change:

110 Quality improvement and total quality

- corrective (e.g. as a result of Quality System problems such as inadequate test records or insufficient document control);
- improvement (e.g. to increase the effectiveness of the products and services, such as reduced product defect rate, faster support service).

The only restriction that the BS 5750/ISO 9001 Standard places on change or improvement is that the Quality System must still be fully documented and comply with the Standard. (It should be remembered that BS 5750/ISO 9001 does not specify directly the level of quality, so it is always possible to improve the quality levels within an existing Quality System.)

Programmes of Total Quality Management (TQM) are common in industry, although as yet less widespread amongst IT suppliers and users (although some IT organisations have made significant progress). Typically, a Quality System leads to Quality Improvement initiatives which in turn lead to adoption of Total Quality as the company's 'philosophy'. A Total Quality approach is usually characterised by strong company-wide emphasis on cultural and people-oriented issues and a strong customer-led view of the quality and effectiveness of its products and services. The company's approach to quality originates from a mission statement of what the company is doing and what it intends to become.

Introducing Total Quality can be easier if a Quality System has already been installed, since there is already a formal statement of Quality Policy, assignment of responsibilities for quality, and proven, documented practice. From the viewpoint of Total Quality, a BS 5750/ISO 9001 Quality System is a first step along the path of quality.

A Total Quality Programme is usually characterised by a brief title such as 'Quality through People', 'Meeting Customer Requirements' or 'Continuous Improvement'. The programme consists of numerous related improvement initiatives, which are driven by the organisation's understanding of its products and its customers' needs. The programme is therefore very specific in detail to the organisation.

The timescale to becoming a 'Total Quality' organisation can be considerable. Introducing a BS 5750/ISO 9001 Quality System may take between one and two years, with a similar period needed for migration to continuous improvement, including the preparation, training and introduction of techniques. However, an organisation which is well prepared (e.g. with established Procedures and retained quality records) can shorten this 'evolution' time. Changing an organisation from one where quality is only noticed by failures and problems to one which 'designs in' a known level and content of quality and continually improves its performance can take five years or more.

However, it is not essential to have a Quality System in order to undertake Quality Improvement or Total Quality Programmes. In organisations where the purchasers of IT products and services are internal (e.g. user departments), a full BS 5750 Quality System may not be felt to be sufficiently worthwhile as a means of meeting a primary objective of user-oriented Total Quality. On the other hand, if the organisation has already achieved considerable progress with a Total Quality Programme, it may seem a retrograde step to have to implement a complete BS 5750 Quality System if required by purchasers in the future. The emphasis on 'static' procedures, project plans and quality records may seem retrograde compared to 'dynamic' continuous improvement. One possible solution is to implement those parts of a BS 5750 Quality System which are needed to support the Total Quality objective (e.g. inspection practices), with further parts being implemented if Quality System Certification is needed in the future.

However, the trend to more formal purchaser-supplier relationships between IT departments and their user departments (e.g. using Service Level Agreements and internal contracts) may make a full BS 5750/ISO 9001 Quality System more desirable in the future, particularly if the IT department is tendering in competition with external suppliers. The Quality System provides a 'yardstick' which can be used by purchasing departments to assess potential suppliers (including the IT department) on an equivalent basis; assessing and comparing suppliers' Total Quality programmes is much more difficult – there is no 'Total Quality' equivalent of BS 5750/ISO 9001.

A quality improvement programme

One relatively easy way of introducing quality improvement for IT work is to realise that the defects found by quality control techniques such as inspection and testing indicate where change is needed or improvement can be made. Primarily, inspection and testing ask the question "what is wrong?"; the next step is to ask "why is it wrong?" and "how can we stop it from happening again?". In effect, quality control is widened from being a process of finding defects into a process of ensuring that they do not happen again – it now includes a 'cause and effect' approach to detecting the sources of poor quality.

The concept of quality control can now be widened, so that the product is assessed against pre-defined (and preferably quantified) targets such as system availability or response time. If the target is not achieved, then either the product itself or the process which generates it needs improvement (or the target needs to be reconsidered). Hence, the improvement process is a supplementary process to inspection and testing, assessing the importance and feasibility of potential improvements which have been identified by the defects found. Corrective action or quality improvement teams are constituted to consider and progress the change within defined timescales and to agreed costs. The 'earned value' of the improvement is the cost savings, increased productivity or business advantage brought about by the change.

Managing quality improvement

Running a quality improvement programme requires more than just techniques – the right culture must be established for the programme to be effective. This means:

- Commitment to Quality: there must be full management commitment to the programme which originates at the highest levels of the organisation and continues all the way down (this is easier to achieve if a Quality System has been implemented since this has already required senior management commitment to quality).

- Quality Responsibility: this is assigned and is known. In particular, problems are 'owned' by the relevant individual (an existing Quality System helps to establish these responsibilities for quality). The principle is that everyone is responsible for the quality of the task they perform and hence their contribution to the product or service – this cannot be 'delegated' to others (such as a QA department). Equally, they are allowed to contribute to improvement initiatives, for example by suggesting changes to the procedures or methods they use.

- Product Information: this is obtained from the customers or users to demonstrate the impact of the product's quality and the consequences and costs of any problems. A Quality System helps to provide this information by means of the quality records it generates.

- Failure Information: there are processes for determining the cause of failures and for making appropriate changes to the methods and processes.

A BS 5750/ISO 9001 Quality System prepares the ground for managing quality improvement in this way. A quality policy and corresponding responsibilities will have been established, procedures and standards for the working processes will have been defined, and basic quality records will have been established. During the introduction of the Quality System, a Steering Group or similar body is likely to have been set up – the same group or a closely related one can drive the improvement programme.

Methods for quality improvement

Each task within a Quality Improvement initiative needs to be controlled, to ensure that it is addressing specific problems or targets of improvement and that it is progressing to a conclusion in a reasonable time-scale. A simple approach is to divide each improvement into four steps of a cycle: Plan, Do, Check, Action, where each step is a stage of progress for an individual problem (Figure 8.1).

Methods for quality improvement 113

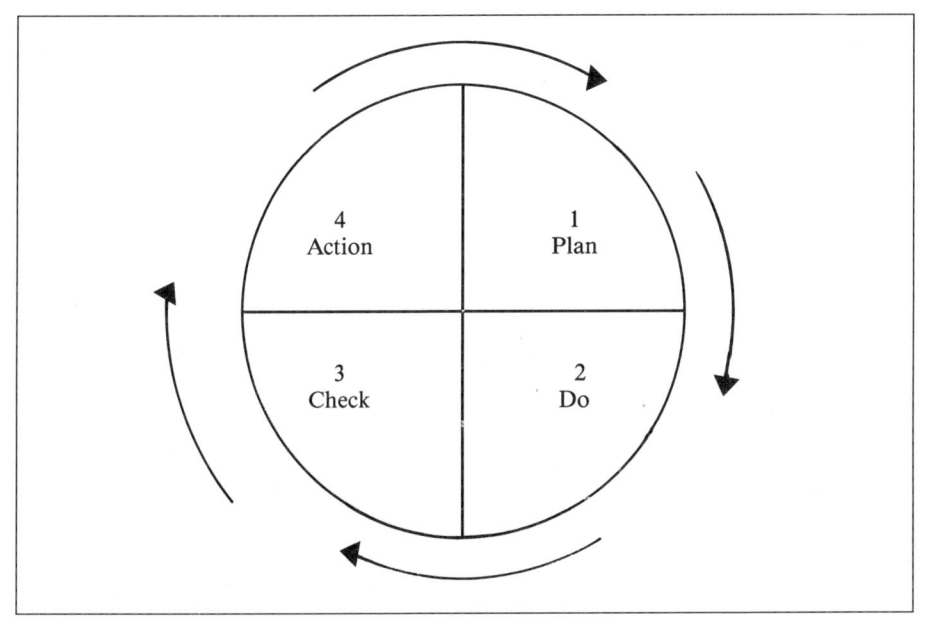

Figure 8.1 Cycle of quality control and improvement

The 'Plan' step

This step defines the problem to be tackled, or the goal to be achieved (e.g. average reported failure rate of five per week to be reduced to no more than two). This step also defines the context of the problem, e.g. unacceptably low system availability for the user and excessive support costs for the supplier. (If the improvement offers benefits to both supplier and user, it may be appropriate to involve both in the improvement task.)

The 'Do' step

This step concentrates on identifying the likely solution to the problem ('what has to be done?'), including an analysis of why the failure occurred. This requires tracing back the series of effects and causes until the root cause can be identified (i.e. at the level that a solution can be applied).

A 'Fishbone' diagram helps to display the 'chains' of cause and effect and so to trace the root cause (or causes) of a particular problem (Figure 8.2). It is useful to group causes into categories of: Man, Method, Machine and Material.

'Man' means the workmanship of the personnel who have produced or developed the product. 'Method' is the processes and procedures used to develop the product (e.g. how effective and appropriate are the procedures?). For software and IT work, 'Machine' will be the development environment

114 *Quality improvement and total quality*

including hardware, supporting tools and utilities used during system development. 'Material' can include elements such as the information (e.g. User Specifications) on which the system content was based and any external or existing software modules incorporated into the system, in other words, anything which is a 'consumable'.

```
                    Cause and Effect Relationship

            Man                 Method
                                                    ┌─────────────┐
                                                    │   Quality   │
                                                    │ Improvement │
                                                    └─────────────┘
            Machine             Material

            Man      = 'Workmanship'
            Method   = Process and Procedures
            Machine  = Development environment
            Material = Information, 'Consumables'
```

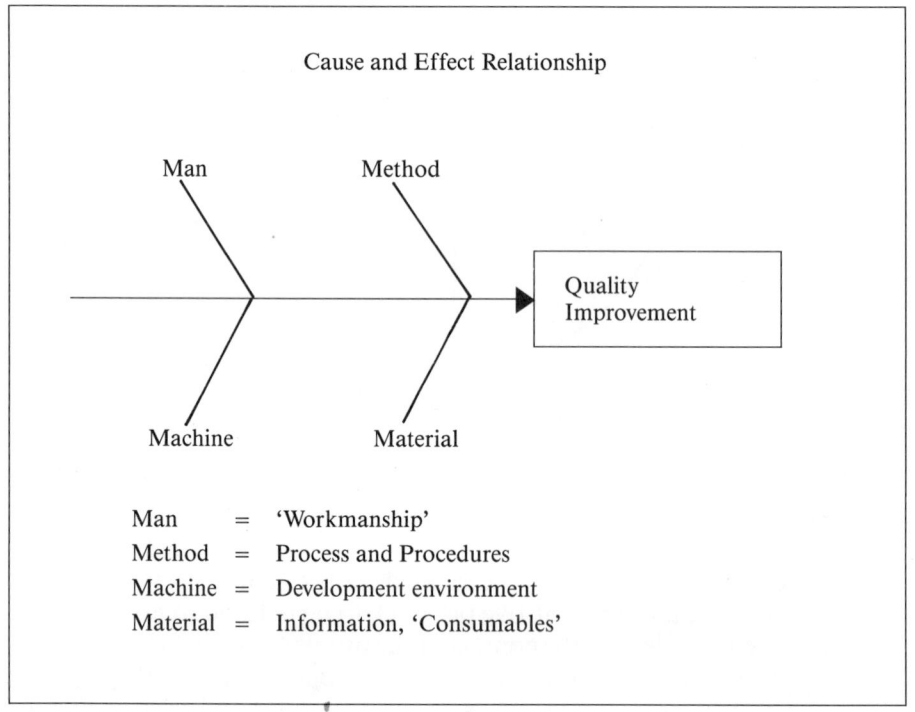

Figure 8.2 The 'Fishbone' diagram

For example, one cause of reported system failure may be improper operation by users – apparently a 'Man' cause. However, this in fact may be due to User Operating Manuals (i.e. 'Material') being out-of-date, incorrect or unclear. In this case, a number of reasons are possible:

– Manuals are not always available because there is no procedure for their circulation at the user installation, and no-one has checked that they have been circulated ('Method' and 'Man').

– They are incorrect and unclear because they have not been validated against actual system operation, and because no users were involved in their review during development ('Method').

There will be several potential solutions to these problems; in the first case, the customer can implement a procedure for circulating and updating User Operating Manuals, and identify who is responsible for carrying it out. In the second case, both corrective and preventative actions are possible:

- A programme of reviews to identify changes and improvements needed to the existing user manuals, involving the developer and the users (corrective).
- Revision of development practice (amendment of procedures) to ensure that the documentation is reviewed both internally and externally before release (preventative).

The 'Check' step

The 'Check' Step determines the effectiveness of the solution(s) against the target for improvement. The cost and impact of the solution needs to be assessed (it may be effective but too costly to implement in regular practice).

For example, a draft procedure for circulating User Manuals is introduced, and the number of user-reported failures monitored. If successful, the reduction is quantified and an estimate of the time and money saved obtained. These savings are assessed against the cost and impact of implementing this procedure permanently.

The 'Action' step

The 'Action' Step implements accepted improvements into regular practice, for example by amending formal procedures or introducing new techniques. In the example above, if the draft procedure proved successful, it is introduced formally into the Quality System.

Note that while it may be possible to envisage further improvement, this does not necessarily mean that it is feasible yet or that the cost is justified. An improvement process usually includes assessment of the extent to which improvements are justified.

Problem-solving techniques

In analysing the causes of problems and identifying suitable solutions, a number of problem-solving techniques are useful. These help both by providing simple but effective ways of analysing problems and assessing suitable solutions and by providing a repeatable, structured method for doing this (which can itself be subject to improvement, if needed).

Brainstorming

This technique is useful at the start of the problem solving process by creating a large number or wide range of ideas in a short space of time, e.g. in this case, the likely causes of the problem. A small group of personnel participate in the process who understand the problem and therefore know the likely causes. A group leader records (e.g. on a flip-chart) the ideas proposed by each member in turn until no new ones are generated or a time limit (e.g. 10 minutes) is reached. There is no comment or criticism, no matter how irrelevant an idea may seem at the time (the technique does not assess the ideas proposed).

For example, a brainstorming session on the reasons for operating problems on a computer system might produce the ideas:

- defective software
- inadequate testing
- misleading user instructions
- untrained operators
- inaccurate specifications
- increased usage of the system
- faulty hardware
- invalid data entered.

A second stage to brainstorming can classify, assess or rank the ideas, as relevant to the problem. In the example above, assessment might include:

- customer or developer responsibility
- likely cost and timescale for solution
- importance or impact on customer
- does evidence exist?

If additional ideas emerge, a further cycle of brainstorming can be attempted. The leader ensures that further cycles generate new or related ideas, so that the further time spent is profitable.

Why-why technique

Once a problem has been identified, likely causes have to be explored. This technique repeatedly asks the question 'why?' and records the answer until the root cause is found (i.e. the level at which a solution can be applied). It can be performed by a small group who have sufficient understanding of the processes involved (it can be a follow-up to a previous brainstorming session). For example:

WHY: Unclear User Manual
    WHY: Not reviewed before delivery
        WHY: Insufficient time and resource
            WHY: Reviews not included in the project plan
                WHY: No recommended set of project reviews
                    WHY: Incomplete project planning standards
        WHY: No review method or procedure for user documents
            WHY: Inadequate quality control standards

The Why-Why Technique tends to be divergent, since it will often reveal wider root problems than the initially evident one. Also, it may reveal more than one contributory problem (as in the example above).

How-how technique

This technique is useful for exploring alternative solutions to a problem. It is a convergent process since it identifies specific solutions. For example:

HOW: Reduce system defects
    HOW: Adhere fully to testing plans
        HOW: Independent validation of performance of test plans
        HOW: Include independent validation in project planning standards
    HOW: Perform inspections on all specifications and designs
        HOW: Define and introduce inspection method
            HOW: Pilot inspection method
        HOW: Include inspections in project planning standards

Again, there may be more than one solution available; each 'root' solution must be assessed. In some circumstances, not every solution may need to be feasible for sufficient improvement to be possible.

Force-field analysis

When an improvement is to be made, there will be factors or 'forces' which either assist or resist the change. Force-Field Analysis identifies and assesses the forces according to whether they assist or resist, and for their anticipated 'strength' (e.g. low, medium and high – in the latter case, specific action will be needed to counter them if they are resisting). A strategy for implementing the improvement can be devised which takes into account these forces, their direction (for or against) and their relative strengths.

118 Quality improvement and total quality

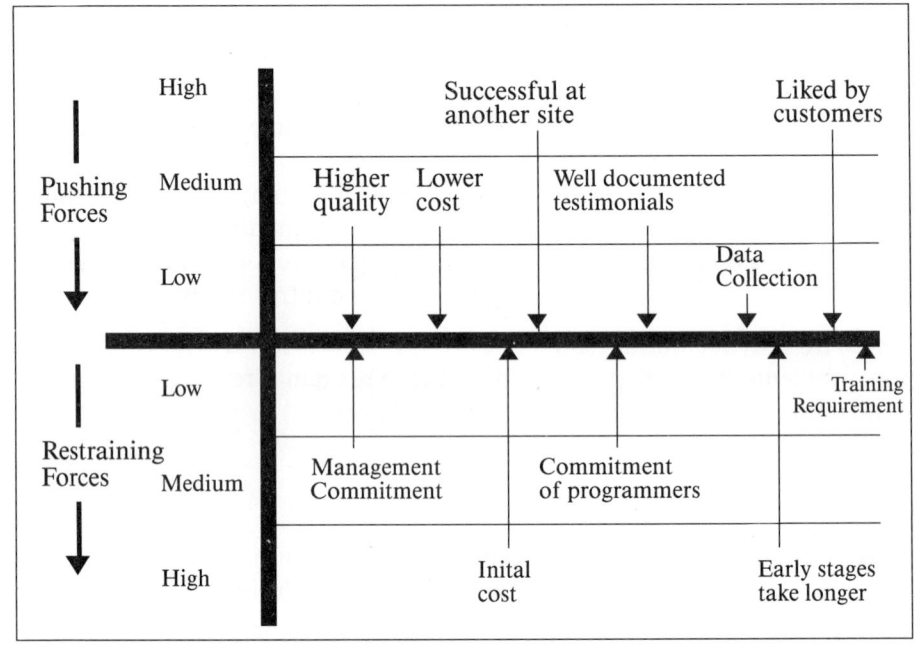

Figure 8.3 Force-field analysis: Introducing inspection

The strength of a factor can be assessed against guidelines such as:

- LOW: will require little effort or few measures to obtain/counteract. Unlikely in itself to achieve/prevent objective, but will be an influence.
- MEDIUM: will require specific measures requiring noticeable cost or effort. Represents significant assistance/resistance to the objective.
- HIGH: will require substantial measures, and related cost/effort. Will be a powerful influence on achieving/preventing the objective.

Quality costs

A good starting point for a quality improvement programme is the potential cost savings. It is often stated that between 20% and 30% of a company's turnover is wasted by poor quality and its consequences, such as rework, inefficiency and delayed deliveries. The payback from quality improvement comes from progressively reducing and eliminating this 'waste'. It is still not unusual to hear of IT managers who claim to spend as much on maintenance and support of systems as on their development.

An improvement programme needs to know what savings and costs are involved in any particular initiative to ensure that the potential value of the

Quality costs 119

proposed change is known. (An important driving factor in any change is reduction in costs or better value for money.) The costs associated with product and process quality can be classified as:

- failure (internal and external)
- appraisal
- prevention
- opportunity.

As a company handles quality more effectively, the quality costs which it recognises will tend to move through these categories. Initially it will be aware of failure costs, in particular rework and correction (and possibly rejected products). These failure costs will be both internal (incurred by the developer) and external (affecting the purchaser or user). They are 'negative' in that they add directly to supplier costs (and often user costs as well) and reduce margins and profits for both supplier and purchaser.

Failure also results in costs of lost opportunity, since personnel and other resources are prevented from being productive by the time spent on corrective work to existing products. Loss of business, goodwill and reputation are other forms of lost opportunity.

When the extent of failure costs is realised, it will lead to more time and effort being spent on appraisal, for example by perfoming more inspections, testing and other forms of quality control. For IT work, appraisal can be particularly effective by finding errors early (e.g. at design rather than at system testing) when they are much cheaper to correct.

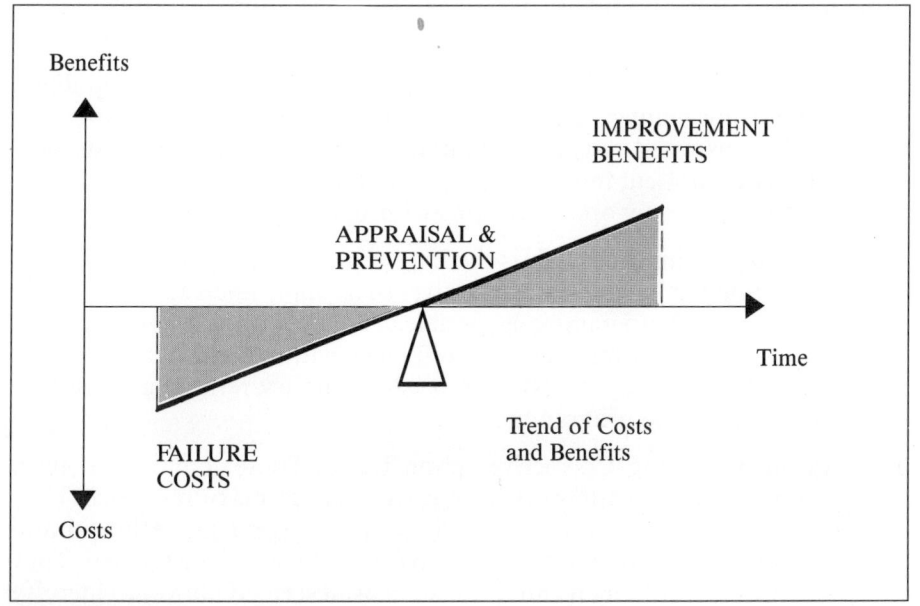

Figure 8.4

Appraisal may show that several basic reasons (e.g. inadequate project planning procedures) are at the root of many problems or are a common contributing factor. This leads to the realisation that money spent on prevention (e.g. reviewing and improving procedures) will reduce appraisal and failure costs (Figure 8.4). The aim, of course, is to produce benefits which significantly exceed the cost of prevention measures. The benefits of eliminating errors before they happen is twofold; not only is productivity increased (because less time, cost and resource is spent on appraisal and correction), but a better product is produced.

One of the aims of an improvement programme can include altering the balance of quality costs – instead of incurring uncontrolled and recurring failure and opportunity costs, the money and resource is invested in appraisal and prevention (and eventually improvement). To demonstrate this is happening, knowledge of what these costs are is essential – one benefit of a Quality System is that failures are identified, and often with at least some of their failure costs being known.

A Quality Costs Initiative is often one of the first steps beyond a BS 5750/ISO 9001 Quality System, since the Quality System has made costs easier to track and knowledge of these costs is one of the basic requirements for managing a Quality Improvement or Total Quality Programme.

A typical improvement programme

Whether aimed at improvements to the Quality System or a wider Total Quality Programme, a typical Quality Improvement Programme will include the following elements:

1. Management Commitment. The overall programme operates top-down from senior management, only moving on when previous achievement has been assessed and their support has been obtained for the next stage. This commitment must be apparent to all personnel (e.g. by a Policy Statement and by open reporting of progress and decisions).

2. Steering Committee. This is the long-term 'governing body' which is constituted to include representatives of as many levels and viewpoints affected by the programme as possible. It defines policy, reviews progress, and agrees targets and terms of reference within the programme (e.g. for problem-solving teams). Membership can vary, reflecting the current emphasis of the programme.

3. Problem-Solving/Corrective Action Teams. These mainly short-term teams are set up with specific objectives and terms of reference. They should include representative mixes of management, technical and support functions as appropriate to the problems being tackled. They use problem solving techniques (such as described above) to identify and propose solutions.

A typical improvement programme

4. Awareness and Training. It is vital to promote (and maintain) awareness of the programme through means such as posters, newsletters, articles and meetings. Cultural change in personnnel attitudes can be difficult and may require substantial (but essential) initiatives. Full understanding, commitment and support of personnel to the programme is the aim.

   All staff should be trained in basic techniques of quality improvement and problem solving, since everyone is likely to be involved in an improvement initiative at some time.

5. Quality Requirements and Objectives. The programme must make clear what the quality objectives are – typically they are based on meeting customer expectations, but often internal productivity and effectiveness as well. If aims such as 'Zero Defects' are stated, it must be clear whether these are long-term, to avoid too much being expected too soon. The aims must be reflected in the emphasis of the programme, e.g. towards eliminating defects in products and services and improving them further, and therefore involving substantial contact with the customers and users to help in understanding their needs better.

6. Quality Information. To demonstrate the nature and extent of problems (and, importantly, the subsequent achievement of improvement), information (preferably quantitative) relating to initiatives must be obtained and made available. This can include, for example, lists of outstanding quality problems, their costs and impact; and subsequently the results of improvement, the cost savings and benefits achieved. This helps greatly to demonstrate confidence in the programme's achievements.

All these principles can be applied to IT and software work – and typically once the first major improvement initiative, the introduction of a Quality System, has been achieved. The Quality System helps directly to establish the kind of culture and practices needed to move into full programmes of Quality Improvement and Total Quality.

Appendix 1
Configuration management

Introduction

Software and IT work requires Configuration Management — the identification, control and tracking of all the items which constitute the software product and all the versions of these items. (In many cases, hardware items need to be included as well.)

The more intangible nature of sofware, the amount of related documentation and the apparent ease with which changes can be made are some of the factors which can make software Configuration Management difficult to achieve. Also, the scale and complexity of larger software projects does not always help. The benefit to be achieved is effective product control — we know how the software is built, which versions of items form a product release, how the software is related to its documentation, what changes have been made to the items, and we can check that the software is the version which was intended.

While Configuration Management might not be thought of as a quality control activity, lack of the product control it provides can result in significant quality problems, such as:

- the wrong version of user documentation is released;
- program changes are made without authorisation or any consideration of the effects elsewhere (e.g. on design and operation);
- the effect on the software of a requirements change cannot be clearly identified;
- the master version of a software module cannot be obtained;
- a program was used in a software release before it had been fully tested and approved.

As with many quality-related activities, the need for Configuration Management tends to become apparent only when these types of problem arise, by which time it has become difficult or impossible to institute the controls which should have been applied from the start.

Configuration management and quality standards

The BS 5750/ISO 9001 Standard makes no explicit mention of Configuration Management, but it is implied by a number of the Standard's requirements;

- design control, including the identification, documentation and approval of design changes;
- document control, including approval, issue and the handling of changes and modifications;
- product identification and traceability;
- identification of inspection and test status;
- control of non-conforming product.

Configuration Management is included in the ISO 9000-3 interpretation; this means that, for software and IT work, it is a recognised means of meeting the requirements of the BS 5750/ISO 9001 Standard which are listed above.

What is configuration management?

Any project or operation requires a set of controls which (in software terms):

- uniquely identifies every module, document and system created and released. (These identified items are often termed Configuration Items.);
- ensures the retention and safe custody of the items and control of the issue and distribution of copies;
- identifies, records and controls all changes to these items;
- monitors the status and history of each item as it is developed, modified and used.

Configuration Management also allows system completeness and correctness to be verified to the extent of checking that the items required are available (e.g. fully tested) and are the right version; for example that a system build is complete and is the one defined. (This does not replace the need for verification or testing of software items; this should be a prerequisite of an item being accepted into the Configuration Management System.)

In practice, Configuration Management may be achieved for software work by a mixture of solutions. Documents can be held in a specified filing cabinet, with appropriate indexes and records of their distribution. Direct access to these items is limited to a nominated person (such as a Configuration Librarian or Project Librarian). Similarly, completed software items are transferred by project personnel to separately designated files and disks of the development system, to be under the control of the Configuration Librarian (and specifcally not the developer).

If preferred, documentation can be held on machine, with similar controls on access (if held in both 'soft' and 'hard' forms, it must be clear which version is the master). However implemented, the set of product control methods forms the 'Configuration Management System'.

The set of master Configuration Items, whether software or documentation, are held in a Project Library or Repository from which all authorised copies and builds are made, under the control of the Librarian. This ensures the integrity and safe keeping of the masters and is the only source of copies. Depending on project requirements, this Library may be a centralised function for all projects, or a specific project activity (or even a mixture). The Project Librarian/Configuration Librarian task is primarily one of technical administration, and is best performed by someone who is independent of the development work.

A basic Configuration Management System can be provided by maintaining (in the Project Library) an 'Items List' which identifies each Library item and includes information such as date of entry, authority and status; and a "Library Log" which records the history of each item while in the Library. Other relevant information can be added as necessary.

A configuration management system

A full set of Configuration Management procedures provides the following forms of control (see also Figure A1.1).

Version control (identification control)

This identifies each item and records its history of development, including incorporation in successive builds, versions and releases. Item masters must be stored and capable of retrieval, for example, if a previous build needs to be restored because a new version proves to be unsuccessful. Version control may need to allow for the creation and co-ordination of different variants of items or builds (e.g. concurrent versions of the product for different customers).

Build control

This controls the building of software from component items (including associated documentation). This aspect of Configuration Management can

126 Appendix 1

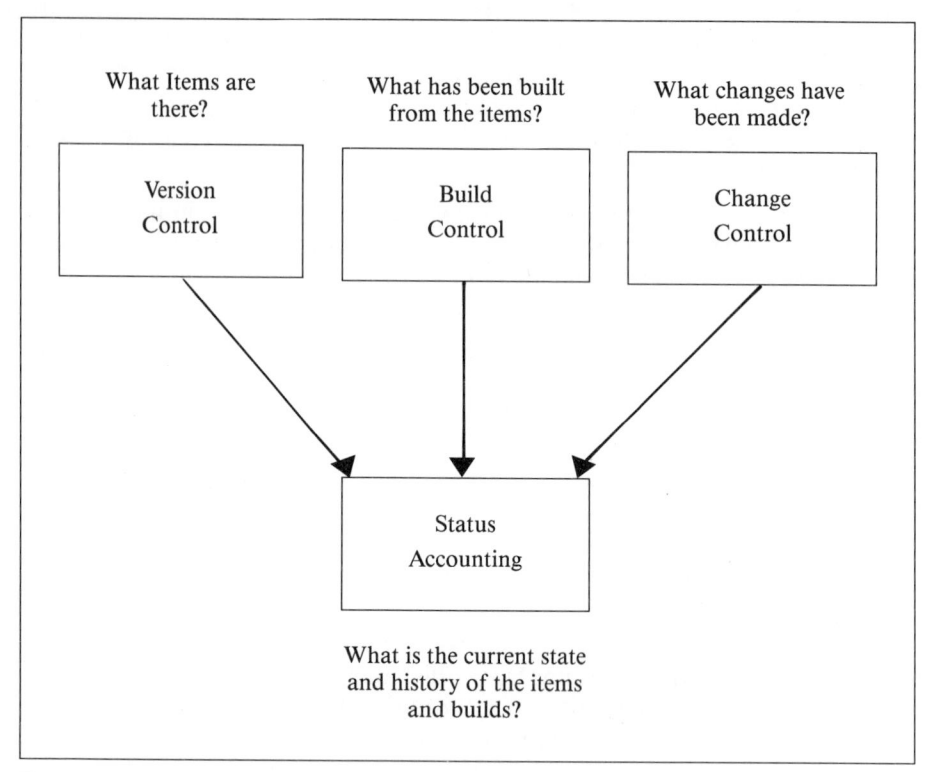

```
┌─────────────────────────────────────────────────────────────┐
│                                                             │
│  What Items are      What has been built    What changes have│
│     there?           from the items?         been made?     │
│                                                             │
│   ┌─────────┐         ┌─────────┐          ┌─────────┐      │
│   │ Version │         │  Build  │          │ Change  │      │
│   │ Control │         │ Control │          │ Control │      │
│   └─────────┘         └─────────┘          └─────────┘      │
│           \                │                  /             │
│            \               │                 /              │
│             ↘              ↓                ↙               │
│                      ┌───────────┐                          │
│                      │  Status   │                          │
│                      │ Accounting│                          │
│                      └───────────┘                          │
│                                                             │
│                    What is the current state                │
│                    and history of the items                 │
│                          and builds?                        │
└─────────────────────────────────────────────────────────────┘
```

Figure A1.1   Forms of control

benefit considerably in integrity and productivity from the use of Configuration Management tools (see below).

Change control

This is the control of change to items (including authorisation) and in particular to product releases. Also, during development, the completed set of products at the end of a project phase can be established – the term 'Baseline' is often used to represent this product set. A Baseline is a product version which is significant during its development or evolution, such as the complete software design or a fully tested system.

Status accounting and reporting

The information held by the Configuration Management System allows the status and history of each item and product build to be monitored. This is important, in particular so that the completeness and validity of a release can be checked and so that the Configuration Management System can be audited.

Part of the preparation for a release should be a configuration audit to confirm that the specified build of valid items has been performed.

Change control can be preceded by a defect report control (or problem reporting) procedure which receives and assesses information on suspected system faults. As well as responding to the originator (e.g. to confirm recognition of the defect or to request further information), it passes genuine problems on to change control for consideration and authorisation. Also, the output from defect report control provides the best point from which to determine the actual defect rate of the product (Figure A1.2).

The combination of defect report control and change control can provide the basis for management of the maintenance and support of the system once it is operational, since the same processes are required.

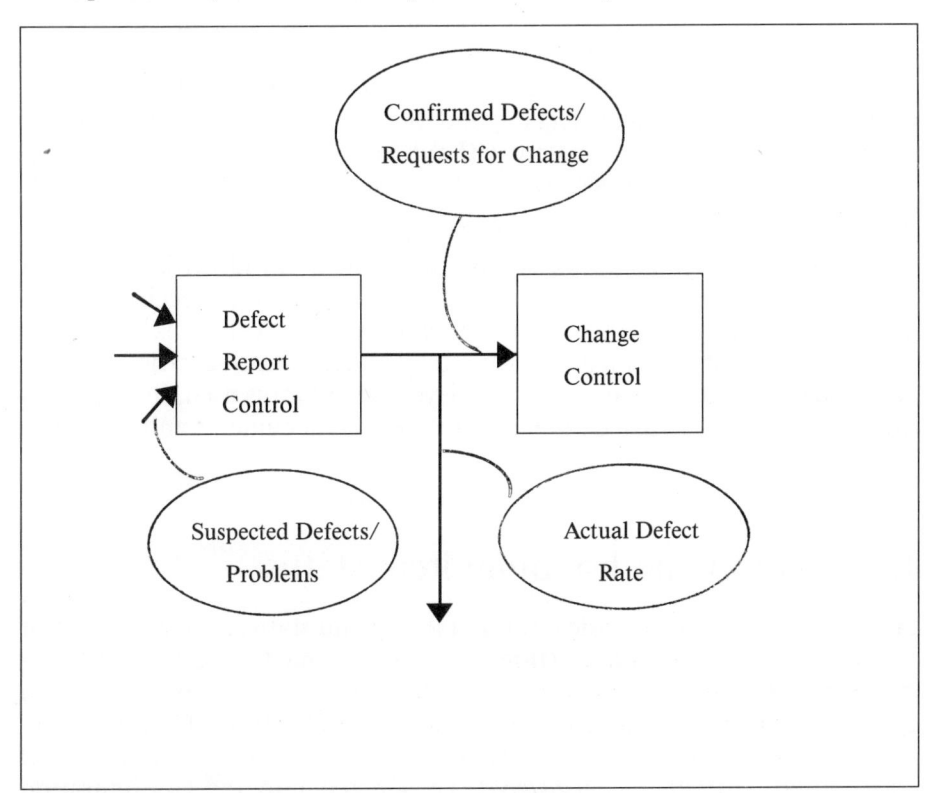

Figure A1.2 Defect report control and change control

A Configuration Management System should include identification of the utilities, support software and other facilities used during development, such as Operating System, Compiler, other software tools and hardware details, if relevant. An important potential requirement is the regeneration of software builds, particularly if any masters are lost or previous versions need to be regenerated.

Configuration identification

Every item which a project produces or uses needs to be identified uniquely. There must be a unique identifier for all project items, including:

- software modules
- documents (including specifications, designs, plans, project records)
- system builds and versions
- system releases.

The number and variety of configuration items for a typical software project can be considerable; it is well worth investigating these requirements as early as possible during project planning, to ensure that the identification system will be adequate for project requirements and that the Configuration Management System will be adequate. The Configuration Librarian co-ordinates the issue of identifiers (a good identification system should allow most identifiers to be generated without intervention, e.g. by including identifier fields for the project, phase type of item and, possibly, the author's name as well).

The ISO 9000-3 Guidelines include a requirement for identification of all software items throughout the development life-cycle from specification to delivery (and afterwards if required by the contract). Traceability is important, in particular identification of the functional and technical specifications for each version of an item, as well as the development tools used, interfaces to other software and hardware items and all related documents and computer files.

Registration and bonding: item status

A useful practice which indicates the stability and status of items is that of 'Registration' and 'Bonding' (Bonding is also termed 'Freezing'). During development, item changes may be too frequent and unpredictable for the item to be held in a Project Library and so it is not handled by the Configuration Management System. However, when the item has been completed and successfully verified it is *registered*, i.e. entered into the Configuration Management System. Importantly, this means that it is now 'owned' by the project, not the author.

In the registered state, further changes to the item are possible (e.g. as a result of integration work or interface changes) but should not be expected at the time of registration. Changes require similar authorisation to that required for first registration, e.g. from the Project Manager, Team Leader or Quality Engineer, depending on the importance of the item to the project. A registered item is not available for delivery or external use, although it can be used within the project.

Registration can also be used to provide project custody of an item, for example, if work on an item is interrupted for a period or the person working on it is changed. This helps to protect the item from loss or corruption and so maintains its integrity.

Bonding

When a registered item has been fully tested or reviewed and is authorised as suitable for incorporation in a release, it is bonded (or frozen) and therefore subject to full Configuration Management (including change control) procedures. Changes must now be formally requested, assessed and approved, for example, by the Project Manager and the Quality Manager and, if relevant, the customer or user representative. (A Change Control Board which includes these roles is recommended for this purpose.) The Configuration Librarian implements a change only on evidence of authorisation from the Change Control Board or equivalent authority.

In a sense, bonding makes change deliberately difficult, to ensure the integrity of deliverable products and to restrict the extent of change. There must be every confidence that the item is complete, stable and suitable for delivery before it is bonded, since subsequent change may take considerable time and effort to achieve.

A documentation system

A project needs a structure for its documentation, just as for its software products, to identify the documents produced and the relationships between them and with the software items.

The set and structure of technical documents should be derived from the life-cycle model and associated technical methods, while project control and quality documents will be determined by the project management and quality management methods. Additionally, there will be project-independent documents such as the Quality System Procedures and Standards.

A typical project documentation set will include:

- Development documents, from Specifications through Designs to Test Specifications and Integration Plans.

- User Manuals, Operating Guides and other deliverable supporting documents.

- Project Plans, Progress Records, Review Reports and other project management documents.
- Quality Plans, Inspection Records, Test Plans and Results and other quality-related documents.

The extent to which these are deliverable will depend on the nature of the project and the requirements of the purchaser. For example, if the purchaser wishes to maintain or modify the product, documents such as Test Specifications and Build Records will be deliverable items. While all these documents will have to be Configuration Items, it must be clear which are available externally or only internally.

The ISO 9000-3 Guidelines identify relevant documents for control to be:

- procedural documents (i.e. those which define the Quality System);
- planning documents (relating to the project);
- product documents.

The document set for a technical item should include (as appropriate to the item):

- the development phase input (e.g. design information for a program);
- corresponding phase output documents (e.g. the design documentation itself);
- test or verification plans and results;
- external (purchaser and user);
- information maintenance documentation.

Controls required

The controls applied to project documentation need to include:

- identifying those documents which come within the system (e.g. a designer's working documents do not, but the design documentation will);
- review and approval of documents before issue;
- update of documents and withdrawal of old versions;
- change control, including review and approval.

These controls will be implemented by a corresponding set of document control procedures.

Configuration management plans

One of the early tasks of project planning should be the production of a Configuration Management Plan. This includes information such as:

- project team responsibilities, including specific roles of individuals;
- operation of the Project Library, including responsibilities and authorities for entering items, their safe custody and access to them;
- configuration item definitions and status, in particular, which development items (including documentation) are to be placed under configuration control and when;
- identification of project baselines and releases and corresponding Configuration Management requirements, including audits and authorisations;
- change control procedures and responsibilities (this may include a Change Control Board, particularly in the case of a bespoke development for a customer);
- configuration records, their retention and custody.

The content of a full Configuration Management Plan is described in the Standard ANSI/IEEE 828, "IEEE Standard for Configuration Management Plans".

Configuration management tools

The nature of software makes the use of tools for Configuration Management attractive, particularly for tracking the relationships and traceability between items and for handling access to Configuration Management records and to the Project Library (e.g. from project team members who have different access requirments). Links with the development system to prevent invalid system builds being attempted is another potential advantage.

Configuration Management tools may need to be large and complex to support the needs of large developments; on the other hand, a database package may be able to provide a degree of useful support for a small or simple project.

A Configuration Management tool aims to assist and automate the entry, access and analysis of configuration information. Most tools are implemented around a database which has been adapted or designed for the purpose. Many operate on VAX/VMS or UNIX development environments. Some points to look for in Configuration Management tools:

- Is the tool general purpose or software-specific? (Software projects involve a wide range of software, hardware and documentation items.)
- Does it preserve unique identification of items, but without restricting the format (e.g. simple item names may not be sufficiently flexible for a hierarchical, design-based, item identifier)?
- Does it allow recording of incremental changes to a baseline where this is appropriate? (This can save on the tool's storage requirements and help control of an evolving product.)
- Does it, as a minimum, allow relationships between items to be recorded (e.g. A is part of B, C is used by D)? These relationships should be available to support the building of versions.
- Can it trace the effects of an item change on related items?
- Does it offer an automatic building facility or assistance in generating builds which comply with configuration information?
- Can it generate reliable historical information on items or groups of items (e.g. to support Configuration Audits)?
- Does it allow for the entry of externally-supplied items (where information about the item may be limited)?
- Is write-access to the Library strictly controlled, with appropriate levels of authority for read access? (Items and the information about them may need different levels of security.)
- What limits are there to the possible effects of file corruption or machine failure?
- How flexible is the tool to the particular Configuration Management controls and authorities for individual projects?

Summary: the benefits of a configuration management system

A Configuration Management System should ensure that:

- The current state of all project items (software, hardware, documentation) is known and controlled throughout development (and operation if needed).
- Items and builds can be regenerated if necessary (e.g. as a result of disk failure and loss of files). It may be advisable for significant previous builds to be safeguarded.

Summary

- Changes, corrections and enhancements can be implemented under proper controls and authorisation.
- Access to items can be shared (e.g. design items common to several programmimg activities) with suitable controls, and with co-ordination of any changes to these items for those accessing them.
- The state (and status) of items and builds are known, particularly at delivery and at development baselines.
- Documentation versions are appropriate to the software items, and any changes are co-ordinated (note that if a software item changes, associated documentation may not necessarily have to change).
- Particularly after delivery, software problems can be traced back to the component items and any history of change can be obtained.

Configuration Management is an essential practice within a Quality System.

Appendix 2
Life cycle models

Introduction

The concept of the life-cycle model for software and IT development is now widely accepted, and has been extended to other similar work such as application enhancement and software package selection. It is the idea of breaking a large item of work, such as a development project, into a series of phases (or stages). Each phase is as self-contained as possible, with its own products, plans, resources, methods, procedures and standards. The intention is to make projects more manageable and effective by breaking the work down into simpler and more controllable units. This also allows earlier assessment of project progress in terms of phase-by-phase progression, rather than having to view the project as a single, much larger, unit which is much more difficult to assess and control. The benefits for product quality should be obvious.

The term "life-cycle" implies the entire life of a project from conception, through development and operation to phaseout. In practice, developers often use the term to cover their development part of the life-cycle, excluding the early and late phases with which they have little or no involvement, such as Feasibility Study and Operation. However, when both developer and purchaser recognise a single and consistent life cycle, it ensures that there are proper interfaces between 'their' parts of the project and that each other's contribution is better understood.

"Model" implies a complete set of work phases, methods, practices and responsibilities which together provide everything that is needed to create the product and to manage the project (including its quality requirements). The model provides the framework within which the detailed phases are planned, controlled and assessed. At the project level, the model should be understandable not just by suppliers and developers but by purchasers and other external parties. This allows the project to be monitored and assessed by the purchaser, handed over from purchaser to supplier at a defined point (e.g. after initiation) and eventually from developer to user (for operation and maintenance). It represents the 'common understanding' of how the system is defined, developed and operated.

136 *Appendix 2*

From the developer's viewpoint, the life-cycle model is the development strategy, representing its top-level approach to project work. While the simplest approach is a sequential set of phases, several paths of phase may be required in appropriate circumstances, e.g. for a series of sub-system deliveries, or to allow detailed system test specifications to be developed while the software is being coded.

Types of life-cycle model

There is no universal life-cycle model which is applied to IT and software work, but two basic types are commonly used:

- sequential
- cyclic.

Sequential models

This type comprises a series of phases, each of which is largely a self-contained 'mini-project' with defined end-products, methods, resources and control. The phases are usually sequential and represent self-contained steps of technical progression. An example of a sequential set of phases is:

1. Initial Study
2. Requirements Definition
3. System Specification
4. High-level Design
5. Detailed Design
6. Module (component) code and test
7. Build and Integration
8. System Testing
9. User Acceptance
10. Operation and Maintenance

In this example, the supplier (developer)-controlled phases are 3 to 8, while the purchaser (user) phases are 1,2 and 9,10. Collaboration between supplier and purchaser may be required at certain phases (e.g. 3 and 8), while the purchaser can monitor phase-by-phase progress of development (in particular phases 3 to 8) without needing to understand the detailed content of each phase.

Smaller projects may use simpler (fewer phase) models, for example:

1. Initial Study and Authorisation
2. Requirements Definition
3. System Design
4. Module Code and Test
5. Build and Integration
6. Testing and Acceptance
7. Operation and Maintenance

For IT systems work, the stages of Requirements Definition and System Design may be closely linked by the processes of Systems Analysis and Design, with individual requirements being revised as a result of analysis and design work.

Cyclic models

These are particularly useful when a sequential life cycle model is not realistic, for example, because requirements are changing often or the feasibility of a phase needs to be investigated. A significant drawback to a sequential model is that it assumes that a phase can be completed before the next is started, and there will be no rework or change in requirements. A cyclic model allows a series of many short life-cycles, for example by prototyping a solution or method, or adding ('incrementing') another system feature to those already implemented.

A project may require mixtures of several models, for example, a sequential approach to the low risk and stable requirements, and a cyclic approach for the high risk or unstable parts.

Modern development methods such as Fourth Generation Languages (4GLs) allow short development cycles to be undertaken with comparatively little time and effort for each (hours or days rather than weeks or months). Risk is reduced, since it is apparent quickly whether the cycle has been successful. The result after all the cycles have been completed may be the same as if a conventional sequential life-cycle had been followed, but less rework is likely, and any changes to requirements will have been coped with far better because the project uncertainties have been reduced. A drawback may be longer overall development time and more difficulty in managing the project, since longer-term (project level) planning is more difficult.

Defining the project life-cycle

The software life-cycle adopted for a project should be defined in the project plans (in particular the Project Quality Plan). It can be an adaptation of a standard model, a mixture of sequential and cyclic models or whatever combination is most appropriate to the project circumstances. It is useful to establish a set of 'on-the-shelf' standard models for regular project requirements.

Life-cycle models and quality systems

From the point of view of the Quality System, the project life-cycle is the top-level procedure for the work to be undertaken. Each project phase is a step of this procedure, which itself contains lower level tasks, methods and procedures. The BS 5750/ISO 9001 Standard makes no specific requirement for a life-cycle model, but organising a project in this way helps to meet requirements such as:

- contract review,
- design control,
- process control,
- inspection and testing,
- control of non-conforming product,
- delivery,
- servicing;

since the model makes it clear at which phases of the project these are required.

The ISO 9000-3 interpretation states explicitly that a software development project should be organised according to a life-cycle model, including quality-related activities appropriate to the "nature of the life-cycle model used". Requirements relating to individual phases include:

- a development plan to identify the phases, together with their inputs, outputs and verification methods;
- potential problems for a phase are identified and analysed;
- each phase is defined in the plan before it is started;
- phase outputs are verified as meeting the requirements specified at the start of the phase;
- phase outputs include acceptance criteria for subsequent phases.

Development plans will need updating as the project progresses (if only to fill out the detail of the next phase of work); the end of the previous phase is often a convenient time to do this, since tangible products have been completed and an obvious step of progress has been achieved.

Some life cycle models

The waterfall model

The conventional phase-by-phase life-cycle model is sometimes represented as the 'Waterfall' Model because the phases are shown running from left to right down sequential levels (Figure A2.1). It emphasises that the project naturally 'falls' from one phase to the next, in this case with the 'volume' of information and product content increasing with each lower level of phase.

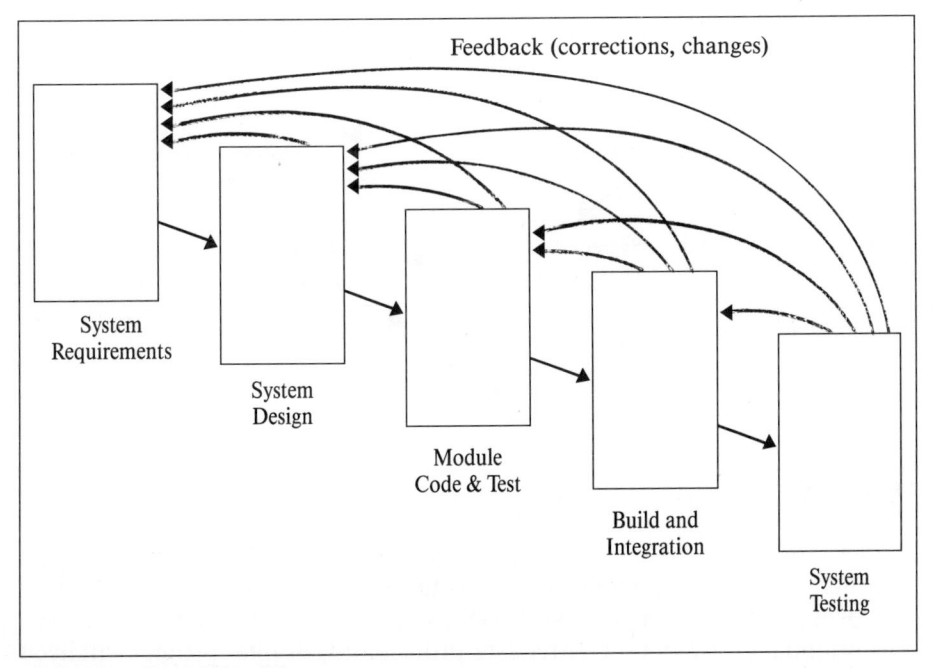

Figure A2.1 Waterfall model

An associated idea is that some of this information flow 'splashes back' to higher (previous) phases, due to changes in requirements, discovered faults or other reasons. There must be some form of project control to minimise (but control) this 'splashback'.

The 'V' model

This is an attractive, two-dimensional, linear model which emphasises the correspondence between earlier and later phases of the project (Figure A2.2). Early phases from top-level initiation down to bottom-level coding and testing are balanced by subsequent integration and test phases rising to top-level operation and eventually phaseout. The approach to testing is based on the results of each integration and build phase being assessed against its corresponding design or specification phase at the same level.

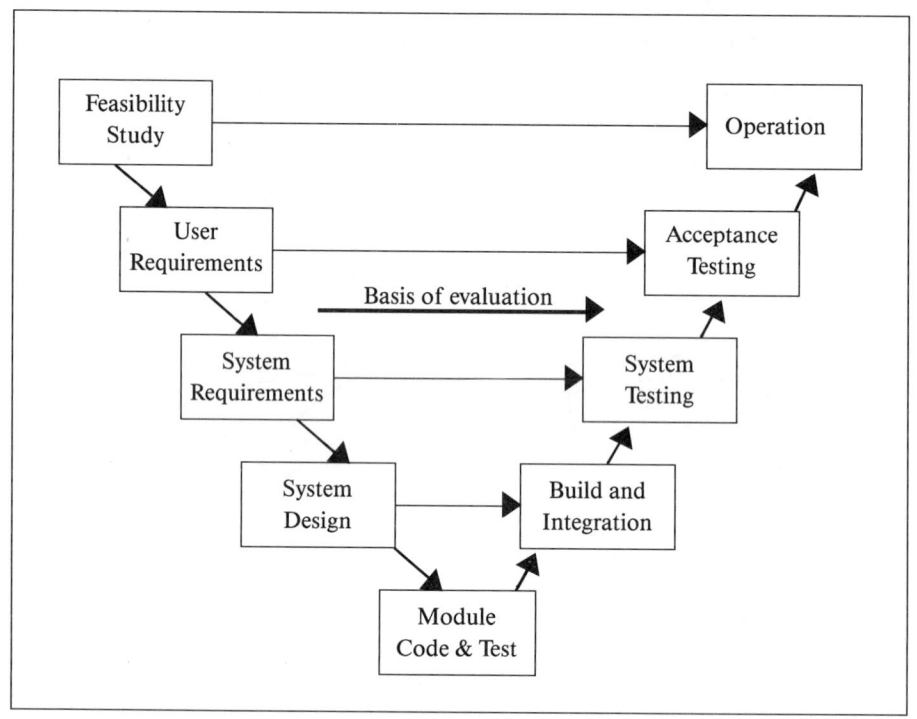

Figure A2.2 'V' model

The model also helps to clarify the involvement of the purchaser and supplier; for example, whoever has produced the specification also defines the corresponding system tests and performs the testing phase at the same level. The boundary between the purchaser project and supplier project will lie at an identifiable level of the model (e.g. between Specification and Design).

Incremental models

If a system is too large for a complete delivery within the required timescale, or some parts are required for early delivery, an incremental approach can be adopted. Typically, the project is broken into two or more 'lines' of development after high-level design, with the resultant increments being implemented cumulatively (Figure A2.3). Each line, with its own sequential phases, may be implemented once the previous one has been completed, or the lines can be overlapped if preferred. In effect, the system is delivered as separate, add-on, increments.

Normally, the complete series of incremental lines will be identified and planned from the start of the overall project.

Evolutionary models 141

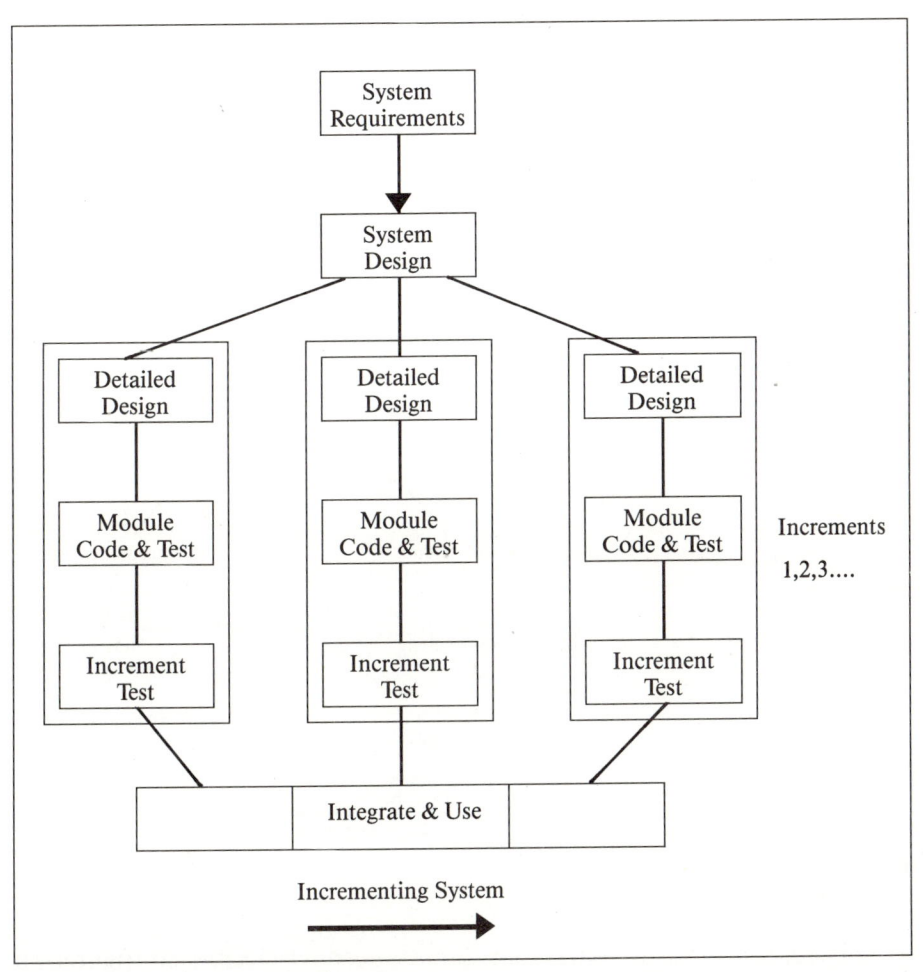

Figure A2.3 Incremental development

Evolutionary models

This type of model caters for regular and even continuous change in system requirements, and allows experience during development and/or operation to be recycled quickly into an amended system (Figure A2.4). It is the opposite to the traditional phase-by-phase life-cycle approach, in that it is intended to cope with changing requirements and short timescales. The system evolves in a series of controlled steps, typically in response to feedback from sources such as system use, development experience or reviews of user requirements. Evolutions can arise for a variety of reasons; for example, they can be incremental (adding further content and facilities), corrective (as a result of detected problems) or innovative (assessing or prototyping new facilities or methods of working).

142 Appendix 2

Evolutionary models require close management, not only to control current evolutions but to identify and assess future evolutions and so maintain a strategic view of the whole system. The attraction is that it can be highly user-oriented, in which case careful co-operation with the users is needed to ensure that their needs are balanced against the feasibility and cost of their provision and the consolidation of the existing system.

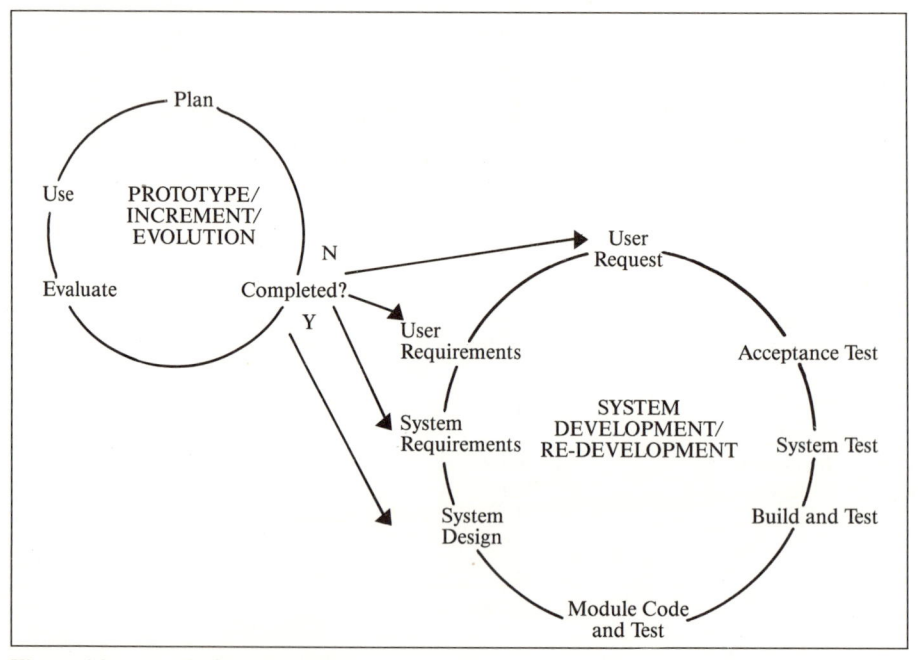

Figure A2.4 Evolutionary model

This approach has its particular quality needs. Effective configuration management is essential, to control the number and variety of system versions, as is verification of each evolution against its requirements. The development methods (which themselves may be being tried out) must still include provision for quality control of their outputs and quality assurance of their effectiveness. The Quality System must include controls (procedures, etc.) to cater for evolutionary methods; in particular a Project Quality Plan or equivalent defining the type of life-cycle approach being followed.

Life cycle models for quality planning

The Life-Cycle Model provides the structure for Quality Plans which identify the methods, procedures and standards, required during the project. Figure A2.5 shows an example of life-cycle intended for IT systems enhancement projects.

Models for quality planning 143

At each phase, the inputs are identified, as well as the Procedures and Standards required. Information (e.g. user comments) will need to be documented, possibly using a pre-defined form.

In a Quality System, a life-cycle chart can be issued as a Standard for each type of project; if necessary, an individual project can adapt it or deviate from it if authorised in a Project Quality Plan. In this example, other models could be defined for alternative situations, e.g. small amendments, new systems development, system support and maintenance. The importance from the quality point of view is that it provides a complete picture of how the work progresses, what procedures and standards apply, and where they apply in the project.

144 *Appendix 2*

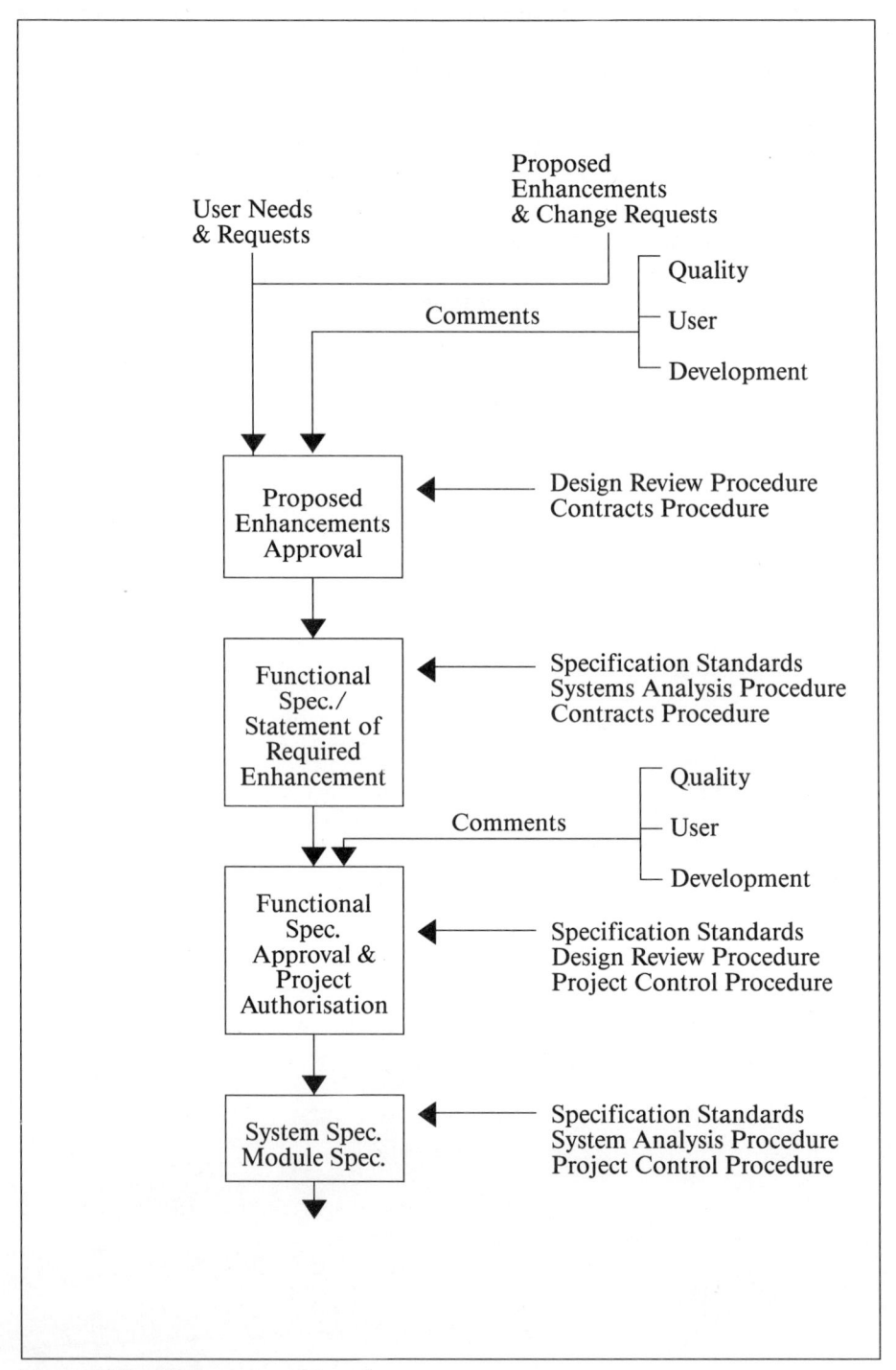

```
                              Proposed
                              Enhancements
       User Needs             & Change Requests
       & Requests
                                            ┌── Quality
                        Comments            │
                                            ├── User
                                            │
                                            └── Development

              ▼         ▼
       ┌──────────────┐
       │  Proposed    │◄──── Design Review Procedure
       │ Enhancements │      Contracts Procedure
       │  Approval    │
       └──────────────┘
              │
              ▼
       ┌──────────────┐
       │  Functional  │◄──── Specification Standards
       │    Spec./    │      Systems Analysis Procedure
       │ Statement of │      Contracts Procedure
       │   Required   │
       │ Enhancement  │
       └──────────────┘
              │                             ┌── Quality
              │                             │
              │         Comments            ├── User
              │                             │
              │                             └── Development
              ▼
       ┌──────────────┐
       │  Functional  │
       │    Spec.     │◄──── Specification Standards
       │  Approval &  │      Design Review Procedure
       │   Project    │      Project Control Procedure
       │Authorisation │
       └──────────────┘
              │
              ▼
       ┌──────────────┐
       │ System Spec. │◄──── Specification Standards
       │ Module Spec. │      System Analysis Procedure
       └──────────────┘      Project Control Procedure
              │
              ▼
```

Figure A2.5a   Enhancement life cycle

Enhancement life-cycle 145

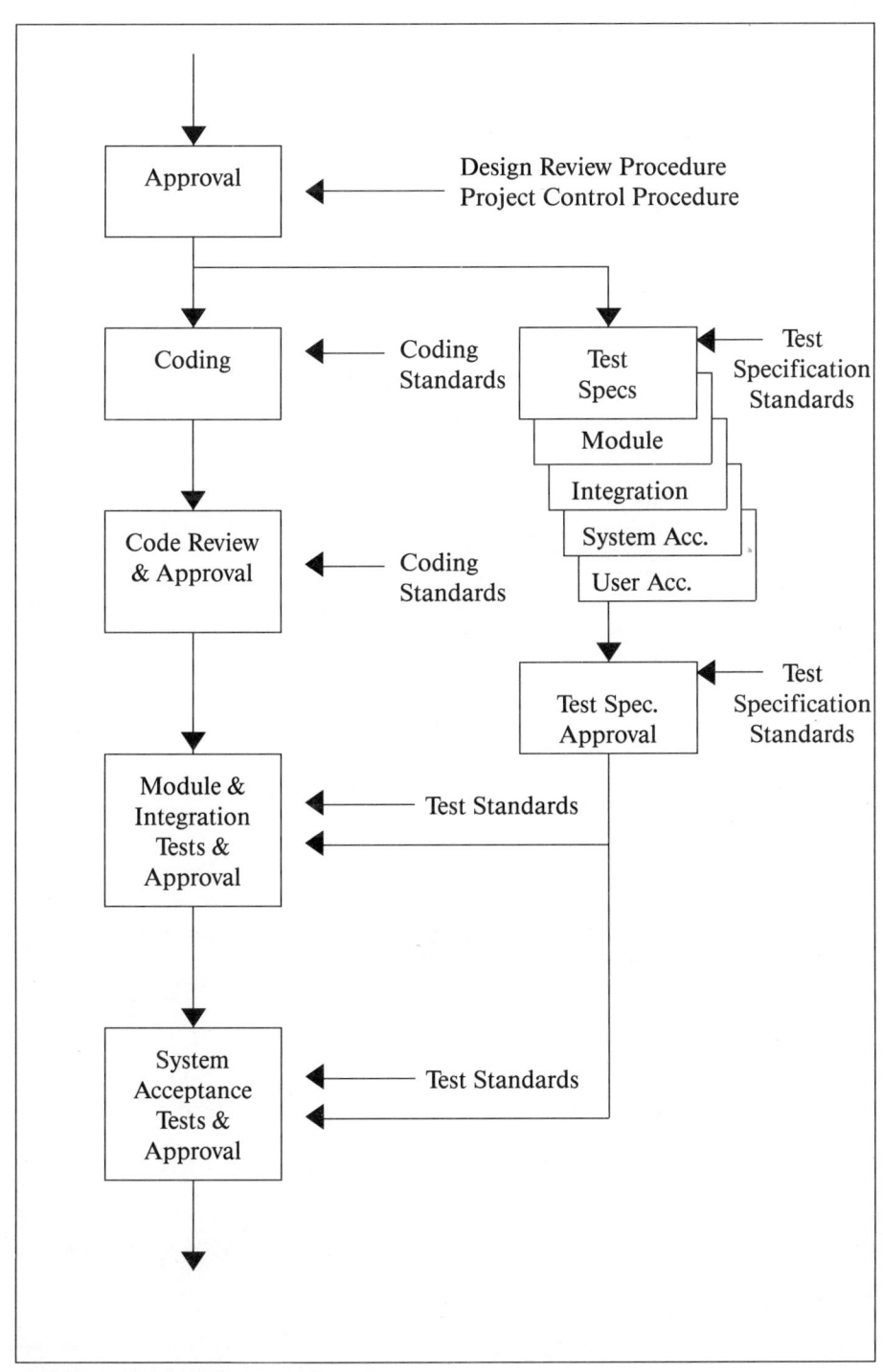

Figure A2.5b Enhancement life-cycle

146 *Appendix 2*

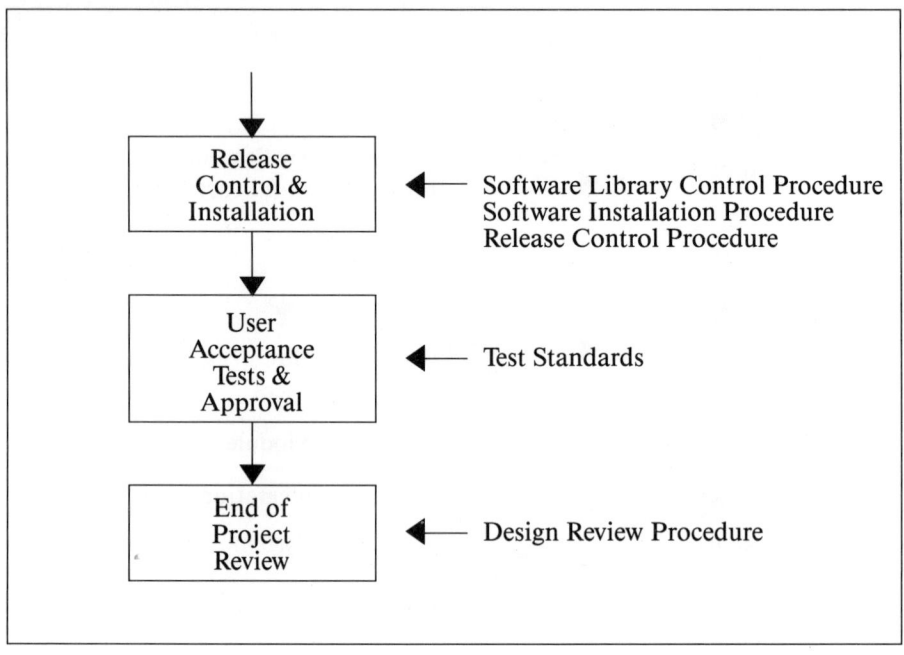

```
        │
        ▼
┌───────────────┐
│    Release    │
│   Control &   │ ◄──  Software Library Control Procedure
│  Installation │      Software Installation Procedure
└───────────────┘      Release Control Procedure
        │
        ▼
┌───────────────┐
│     User      │
│  Acceptance   │ ◄──  Test Standards
│    Tests &    │
│   Approval    │
└───────────────┘
        │
        ▼
┌───────────────┐
│    End of     │
│    Project    │ ◄──  Design Review Procedure
│    Review     │
└───────────────┘
```

Figure A2.5c   Enhancement life-cycle

Appendix 3
Quality records

Collecting information

A Quality System requires the collection and analysis of quality-related information. This provides evidence that the Quality System procedures and practices are being followed and is available to assist problem solving and corrective action. Much of this information is predictable in content and format and therefore is best recorded on pre-defined forms. Examples are:

- Review records
- Inspection checklists
- Audit results.

The BS 5750/ISO 9001 Standard requires quality records to be retained; however, it places little restriction on how these records are formatted and organised. Information or records required include (but are not restricted to):

- *Quality*
  Product quality problems
  Internal Quality System Audit results (including follow-up actions)
  Quality System review results

- *Management*
  Contract Reviews
  Purchaser-supplier meetings and reviews
  Progress Reviews
  Project progress against plan

- *Technical*
  Verification results and corrective actions
  Test results
  Acceptance problems
  Product status
  Product changes

148 Appendix 3

- *Maintenance*
  Maintenance activities
  Problem reports and requests for assistance
  Corrective action priorities and results
  Statistical data on fault occurrences
  Change records

- *Support*
  Current document items and their status
  Product quality data (including metric values, performance)
  Sub-contractor assessment
  Training and personnel experience

As a general principle, there should be records of all procedures followed, tasks performed, and products and items created. There are several ways of producing these records, depending on the scale and complexity of the project and the significance of the information:

- Use of a 'day book' or 'quality log' by personnel to record the work tasks they have performed and related information such as procedures performed, problems encountered, decisions made, information obtained and the outcome of the task, such as test results. The book or log is retained and therefore is available for inspection by appropriate personnel such as the Project Manager, quality assurance staff, etc.

  (This method is particularly relevant for *ad-hoc* information at team member level which would not be held in project-related files, but can be very useful for problem solving. At least minimum requirements for the information required should be formulated.)

- Recording of this project and product information on pre-defined forms designed for the purpose (e.g. Problem Reports). Such forms help to ensure that all required information is recorded and is consistent in content and format between different projects and team personnel.

  This way of recording information is particularly useful for information which needs to be retained by the project, or made available to the customer or for other external inspection (e.g. for quality audit).

- Establishment of one or more Project Files (e.g. Management, Technical, Quality) to hold the relevant project information, preferably on pre-defined forms. These files will normally be in the custody of the Project Manager as they record the project history (and achievement) and provide formal evidence for purposes such as review, acceptance and Quality System audit. The expected structure and content of the Project Files is defined in the Project Quality Plan.

Whichever way these quality records are organised and held, they must provide an 'audit trail', so that, for instance, specific product problems can be traced back or compliance to the requirements of the Quality System can be evaluated.

Designing quality forms

In a Quality System, a balance is needed between the variety and number of forms defined, and the flexibility of content of individual forms. One approach is to first establish a generic form (e.g. Quality Record) which defines the information fields usually needed on most or all types of quality form:

- Scope (e.g. Company/Division/Project)
- Subject (e.g. Inspection record)
- Originator (of the information)
- Approval/Acceptance (as relevant)
- Date
- Content (free format)
- Remarks and Comments (optional)

This form must comply with the Quality System's documentation standards; this typically requires an identifier and/or title, version/issue number and date of issue for all documents. This is to ensure that the form is easily identifiable and that any out-of-date versions can be removed from use. Alternatives should be avoided.

The generic form can be adapted or expanded to meet more specific needs; for example, it can become an Inspection and Review Invitation by adding fields for:

- Project task
- Product/item
- Place and Time
- List of invited attendees and their role
- Inspection criteria

It is useful to include on the form a brief statement of its purpose, particularly if there is any possibility of confusion or misuse. For example: "This Form records the results of a Quality System Audit".

Mandatory and guidance content

The documentation standards must make it clear whether content on a form is mandatory or optional (and therefore included for guidance or recommendation). It is best to be as flexible as possible, for example, by including a field for comments or additional information, and allowing attachment of further sheets if needed. Forms are meant to record and provide information, not to be an end in themselves.

Where a form is used to record information which is of considerable business or contractual importance, such as subcontractor assessment or project stage review, it is clearly desirable to define specific, mandatory, forms for this purpose and to ensure that all information required is recorded.

Checklists

Checklists are a very useful means of supporting review or evaluation activities by ensuring that vital points are covered or that the benefits of past experience are included in the list of questions. These questions record in detail the basis on which the review or evaluation has taken place, i.e. which specific points were covered and what was the result. If necessary, additional questions (which should be within the scope of the review) can be included in the checklist at the time of use. The aim is flexibility of application, so a checklist should indicate which content is mandatory and which is optional or additional.

The quality file

This file contains the forms which are created by the project quality procedures. The records held include:

- Inspection and Review documentation.
- Problem Reports and System Queries.
- Non-conformance reports (including deviations from specification).

These records together enable the current state of the product and its components to be known and record all quality-related activities which have taken place.

Sample quality forms

Quality record

This is the generic form for recording quality-related information, and can be used either as a template for creating specific forms, or as a general-purpose form where no specific one exists (Figure A3.1). If any part of the form is not relevant to the particular use (e.g. authorisation) it is preferable to marked it as "not applicable" rather than being left blank.

```
┌─────────────────────────────────────────────────────────────┐
│  XYZ COMPANY LTD. IT Systems Group                          │
│                                                             │
│                    QUALITY RECORD                           │
│  ┌──────────────┬─────────────────┬──────────┬───────────┐  │
│  │ PROJECT      │                 │ PHASE    │           │  │
│  ├──────────────┼─────────────────┴──────────┴───────────┤  │
│  │ Subject      │                                        │  │
│  ├──────────────┼─────────────────┬──────────┬───────────┤  │
│  │ Originator   │                 │ DATE     │           │  │
│  ├──────────────┴─────────────────┴──────────┴───────────┤  │
│  │                                                        │  │
│  │                                                        │  │
│  │                                                        │  │
│  │                                                        │  │
│  │                                                        │  │
│  │                                                        │  │
│  ├────────────────────────────────────────────────────────┤  │
│  │ Authorised/Reviewed by:                                │  │
│  └────────────────────────────────────────────────────────┘  │
│  Version 1 9/90          Page 1 of 1               QR/QR    │
└─────────────────────────────────────────────────────────────┘
```

Figure A3.1

Inspection and review invitation

This uses the Quality Record form as a basis, but adds to it the specific information needed when setting up an Inspection or Review meeting (Figure A3.2). This form records to which meeting it refers, when the meeting takes place, who should attend and what role is assigned. A master copy of the form can be used to record the actual information at the meeting itself.

The criteria to be applied can be identified more specifically by, for example, reference to the Checklists and Standards applicable to the document which is to be inspected.

The person responsible for authorising the Invitiation (for Inspections, usually the Moderator) will be defined in the relevant procedure.

152 Appendix 3

```
┌─────────────────────────────────────────────────────────────┐
│ XYZ COMPANY LTD. IT Systems Group                           │
│                                                             │
│                      QUALITY RECORD                         │
│                 Inspection & Review Invitation              │
├──────────────┬──────────────────────┬───────────┬──────────┤
│ PROJECT      │                      │ PHASE     │          │
├──────────────┼──────────────────────┴───────────┴──────────┤
│ Subject      │                                              │
├──────────────┼──────────────────────┬───────────┬──────────┤
│ Originator   │                      │ DATE      │          │
├──────────────┴──────────────────────┴───────────┴──────────┤
│                                                             │
│   Place & Time:                                             │
│                                                             │
│   Attendees:   Moderator:                                   │
│                Presenter:                                   │
│                Reviewer(s):                                 │
│                                                             │
│                Assurance:                                   │
│                User:                                        │
│                Other:                                       │
│                                                             │
├─────────────────────────────────────────────────────────────┤
│   Criteria for review:                                      │
│   Product Description                                       │
│   Checklists                                                │
│   Standards                                                 │
│   Quality criteria                                          │
│   Other:                                                    │
│                                                             │
├─────────────────────────────────────────────────────────────┤
│      Authorised/Reviewed by:                                │
├─────────────────────────────────────────────────────────────┤
│ Version 1 9/90         Page 1 of 1              QR/IRI     │
└─────────────────────────────────────────────────────────────┘
```

Figure A3.2

Review checklist

This form adds to the Quality Record a series of checklist questions for the Review (Figure A3.3), in this example evaluating operation of the Project Library. The set of checklist questions is derived directly from the corresponding sections of the Project Library procedure. Each question is framed such that a "yes" answer indicates compliance to the procedure. A "no" answer is normally accompanied by an explanatory note attached to the checklist, and referenced from the "Notes" column. (A note can also explain other answers, such as "Not Applicable" or can qualify a "yes" answer, e.g. "to the extent it was investigated".)

It is important in this case that the form records not just that the review has taken place, but its extent (even if only some of the content of the checklist was investigated) and the grounds for the conclusions reached.

```
┌─────────────────────────────────────────────────────────────────────┐
│ XYZ COMPANY LTD. IT Systems Group                                   │
│                                                                     │
│                    QUALITY RECORD                                   │
│                Project Library Review Checklist                     │
├──────────────┬──────────────────────┬──────────┬───────────────────┤
│ PROJECT      │                      │ PHASE    │                   │
├──────────────┼──────────────────────┴──────────┴───────────────────┤
│ Subject      │ Project Library Review                              │
├──────────────┼──────────────────────┬──────────┬───────────────────┤
│ Originator   │                      │ DATE     │                   │
└──────────────┴──────────────────────┴──────────┴───────────────────┘
```

	Y/N	Notes
1. Introduction 1.1 Is there a Project Library function which holds master copies of all project items, generates items, and controls their release and distribution? 1.2 Is the Project Library the only source of items released to the client or customer? **2. Purpose** 2.1 Is the Project Library performing the tasks defined in Procedure PR/PL? **3. Scope and Applicability** 3.1.1 Is the Project Library Procedure PR/PL applicable to this project without any variation or alternative? 3.2.1 Have all deliverable project items been submitted to the Project Library following successful Inspection? 3.2.2 Are Project Control and Project Quality Files retained in the Project Library? 3.2.3 Have any other items been submitted by project personnel or the Project Manager?		

Authorised/Reviewed by:

Version 1 9/90   Page 1 of 4   QR/CK/PL

Figure A3.3

Notes

This form (Figure A3.4) supplements other Quality Records such as a checklist. The left-hand column is used to number the note, which is in turn referenced from the relevant point in the Quality Record to which it is attached.

Inspection and review report

This form records the outcome of an Inspection or Review, see Figure A3.5. It documents the Moderator's conclusions, and defines the alternative outcomes possible. If the review is incomplete, further explanation would be expected in the "Comments" section. A decision on further action may involve the Project Manager, who can state this decision on the lower section. Signatures represent formal acceptance of the conclusions and outcome of the review.

```
┌─────────────────────────────────────────────────────────────────┐
│           XYZ COMPANY LTD. IT Systems Group                     │
│                        QUALITY RECORD                           │
├───────────────┬──────────────────┬──────────┬──────────────────┤
│ PROJECT       │                  │ PHASE    │                  │
├───────────────┤                  ├──────────┤                  │
│ Subject       │                  │          │                  │
├───────────────┤                  ├──────────┤                  │
│ Originator    │                  │ DATE     │                  │
├───────────────┴──────────┬───────┴──────────┴──────────────────┤
│                          Notes                                  │
│                                                                 │
│                                                                 │
│                                                                 │
│                                                                 │
│                                                                 │
│                                                                 │
├─────────────────────────────────────────────────────────────────┤
│ Authorised/Reviewed by:                                         │
├─────────────────────────────────────────────────────────────────┤
│ Version 1 9/90           Page                        QR/Notes   │
└─────────────────────────────────────────────────────────────────┘
```

Figure A3.4

General points

The use of forms to obtain or record information should be specified by the quality procedures; for example, the Design Review procedure will call for the use of the relevant Checklist. For flexibility, the general Quality Record and the Notes forms can be used to supplement specific forms — the key requirement is to capture and record the information, rather than lose any because the form does not ask for it or does not have room for it.

As well as indicating the version and identifier of the form (as a footer in these examples), it is recommended to use the "Page x of y" convention to ensure that information held on a number of sheets is clearly complete. The Authorisation/Review field will then only be required on the last sheet.

The overall result should be that any Quality Record will indicate by its content:

- what document it is within the Quality System;
- which project/work area it belongs to;
- who raised it or is responsible for it;
- is it complete?;
- is it valid (authorised/reviewed)?;
- is it up-to-date (version, date)?;
- what decisions were made (if relevant)?

XYZ COMPANY LTD. IT Systems Group			
QUALITY RECORD **Inspection & Review Report**			
PROJECT		**PHASE**	
Subject			
Originator		**DATE**	
Review Complete Y/N			
If Review Incomplete Moderator's recommendation for action: Rework/Reconvene/Re-Review/Deem complete /Abandon			
Comments: Signed:			
Project Manager's decision: Signed:			
Version 1 9/90		Page 1 of 1	QR/IRR

Figure A3.5

Appendix 4
Quality related standards

Introduction

This appendix summarises various quality-related standards and guidance documents which are relevant to software engineering. Some are general purpose documents and some are software-specific. There are relatively few standards for software work, so it is useful to know which are available and what use can be made of them.

The documents identified below should be helpful in establishing and operating a software-related Quality System.

Relationship between external software standards and a quality system

The main areas where external standards and guidance material can help to satisfy the requirements of a Quality System are:

- Software Quality Management
- Software Quality Planning
- Configuration Management
- Life-Cycle Documentation
- Verification, Validation and Test
- Methods, Tools and Techniques

Ideally, a standard has a defined method or procedure for achieving it, supported by specific techniques and tools. For internally formulated standards, this can be done fairly readily, for example, by generating an internal procedure or by use of a supporting software tool. Unfortunately, this is rarely possible for external standards; for example, few standards reflect the availability of modern techniques such as Fourth Generation Languages (4GLs).

158 *Appendix 4*

Formal standards from bodies such as the British Standards Institute (BSI) inevitably take time to develop, agree and ratify, and so in a fast-moving area such as software engineering and IT, it is not suprising that they do not always reflect the latest practice. Often it is guidance documents from trade or professional organisations which reflect the most recent practice and understanding.

Available software-related standards generally reflect the following situation:

- reliance on a conventional stage-by-stage life-cycle;
- not specifically related to recent techniques such as prototyping, incremental delivery, use of expert systems;
- no supporting tools;
- little content on risk management;
- no quantitative measures such as metrics or cost of quality.

Internal standards may be needed to address these requirements.

The standards and related documents identified below are likely to be found adequate for current use. New standards and guides continue to be released from time to time. All the documents described below (including defence-related ones) are in the public domain.

Quality management systems

AQAP 1 edition 3 (1984) NATO requirement for an industrial quality control system

This is the general NATO Requirement for an industrial Quality Control System, intended for application to NATO suppliers.

In the UK this Standard has been used for some years by the Ministry of Defence (MoD) for contractor assessment, replacing the earlier MoD Standard DEF STAN 05-21. It is a concise and clear document, although some industrial terms used are not directly applicable to software.

AQAP 2 edition 3 (1984) NATO guide for the evaluation of a contractor's quality control system for compliance with AQAP 1

This document provides guidance for the interpretation of AQAP 1, explaining the terms used and the elements of a Quality System which are likely to satisfy its requirements.

AQAP 13 (1981) NATO software quality control system requirements

AQAP 13 establishes software quality control requirements for contractors, associated with the requirements of AQAP 1. The document is a supplement to AQAP 1 for a software-related Quality System. It can also be used as a guidance document in the application of AQAP 1 to software procurement. It includes software-specific topics not explicitly mentioned in AQAP 1 such as Configuration Management; Tools, Techniques and Methodologies; and Technical Reviews.

AQAP 14 (1984) guide to the evaluation of a contractor's software quality control system for compliance with AQAP 13

This document provides guidance on interpreting AQAP 13 for the evaluation of a contractor's Quality Control System against AQAP 1. It explains each requirement of AQAP 13, and gives examples of its application.

Use of AQAP standards

Use of these NATO Standards by the MoD is now being superseded by BS 5750/ISO 9001 Certification; also MoD second-party assessment is being replaced by third-party assessment (for software) under the DTI-sponsored TickIT scheme.

These NATO documents are in the main clear and concise, although the non-software specific ones sometimes use terms not easily recognisable outside an industrial situation.

BS 5750: Part 1 1987 / EN 29001 (1987) /ISO 9001 (1987) quality systems – specification for design/development, production, installation and servicing

This British, European and International Standard is intended for external QA purposes, primarily to allow a supplier to demonstrate to a purchaser or independent third party that the required elements of a Quality System have been implemented. It is general in application, being concerned primarily with design and development rather than production or manufacture.

This standard is well presented and structured, written concisely, and a noticeable improvement on the previous 1979 version. However, it requires interpretation for specific sectors like software, and some prominent aspects of software work are not directly covered by it, e.g software tools, configuration management, techniques and methods, although they can be inferred from its content.

BS 5750: Part 0 Section 0.1 1987 / ISO 9000 quality systems − principal contents and applications; guide to selection and use

This is a guide to the selection and use of the other Standards in the series (including BS 5750 Part 1/ ISO 9001). QA concepts are defined and the purpose of related documents in the series is explained. It indicates how contract-related review and assessment practices are used to meet the requirements of the Standards.

BS 5750: Part 0 Section 0.2 1987 / ISO 9004 quality systems − principal concepts and applications; guide to quality management and quality system elements (ISO title: quality management and quality system elements − guidelines)

This document describes a basic set of elements from which a general Quality System can be implemented. It explains the importance of the requirements and gives examples of measures to meet them. It is an important document for understanding quality related practice within a Quality System.

ISO 9000-3 Guidelines for the application of ISO 9001 to the development, supply and maintenance of software

This is a guide to applying ISO 9001 to the development, supply and maintenance of software. This is an important document for software and IT work, since it provides a software-specific interpretation of ISO 9001. It includes definitions of software-related terms and divides Quality System requirements into framework (general), life cycle and supporting activities (including Configuration Management and product/process measurement). Cross references to and from ISO 9001 are provided. It supplements and explains the ISO 9001 requirements to provide a much clearer understanding of what a software-specific Quality System should contain.

Other quality system standards

These include:

BS 5882 (1980) Specification for a Total Quality Assurance Programme for Nuclear Installations

MIL-STD-1535A Military Standard, Supplier Quality Assurance Program Requirements

Quality planning standards

There are a number of Standards which assist in the production of quality plans for software development projects. These are practical standards which can be used whether or not a Quality System is in place.

ANSI/IEEE 730:1984 IEEE standard for software quality assurance plans

This Standard defines minimum acceptable requirements for the preparation and content of a Software Quality Assurance Plan. It contains a concise and verifiable set of requirements, based around a conventional life-cycle model. It includes a comprehensive set of Reviews and Audits, including independent Management Reviews.

It is best suited to large or critical developments, and will require scaling down or adaptation to smaller or lower-risk projects which do not justify the full extent of quality planning described in the Standard.

ANSI/IEEE 983:1986 IEEE guide for software quality assurance planning

This very useful Guide explains and clarifies each section of a Software Quality Assurance Plan intended to meet the requirements of ANSI/IEEE 730. It includes checklists to assist the evaluation of a quality plan against the Standard, and explains how to control changes to the Quality Plan.

STARTS purchasers' handbook second edition 1989

This Handbook includes a statement of Project Quality Plan contents within the Quality Assurance chapter, somewhat similar in content to the IEEE Standard. It also describes recommended contractual uses of a Quality Plan.

Configuration management

ANSI/IEEE 828:1983 IEEE standard for software configuration management (SCM) plans

This comprehensive standard defines the content of a Software Configuration Management Plan, including management, activities, tools, supplier control and records. It is verifiable, clear and concise.

162   *Appendix 4*

The Standard is written as a series of requirements, including the setting up of a Configuration Control Board, but needs more detailed procedures and standards in order to implement. It is suited best to large or safety-critical systems development, and may not be easy to scale down to smaller or lower risk projects. It is independent of life cycle or methodology.

EEA guide to software configuration management

(EEA is the Electronic Engineering Association)

This document provides guidance on the principles of SCM, with sections on its application to a project and the use of automated tools. It is a mixture of a general guide to SCM and a requirements standard.(It is not fully verifiable if used as a Standard.) It is based on a conventional life-cycle.

Documentation

BS 5515: 1984 code of practice for documentation of computer based systems

This document provides guidance on the documentation to be produced at each stage of the development life-cycle. It is somewhat out-dated, with implied application to DP work, and usable only for the specific life-cycle, methodology and type of application for which it was written.

ANSI/IEEE 830:1983 guide to software requirements specifications

This is a Guide for writing a Software Requirements Specification (SRS), describing both the content and qualities of a good SRS and including sample outlines. It is comprehensive, covering alternative application areas and development methodologies. It includes a definition of a 'good' SRS and caters for operations and maintenance. While not life-cycle specific, it is not well suited to structured analysis and design methods.

The Guide is clear and consistent with examples and alternative options included. With adaptation, it can provide the basis for an organisation's own standards.

JSP 188 Edition 4: 1987 specification for technical publications for the services

This standard states requirements for documentation associated with the specification, development and in-service support of software for military operational systems. It is a generic standard covering the complete life of a project, but is easiest to relate to a conventional, hierarchical, life cycle model. It may be difficult to display compliance of a documentation system to this standard.

Verification, validation and testing

BS 5887:1980 code of practice for testing of computer-based systems

This Guide deals mainly with test documentation. The approach recommended is based on hardware rather than software requirements. It is intended to complement the documentation standard BS 5515. While independent of a specific life-cycle or methodology, it is not suitable for modern approaches (4GL, knowledge-based systems).

ANSI/IEEE 829:1983 standard for software test documentation

This Standard defines the purpose and content of a set of test documents and provides an outline and examples of their use. It is clear and consistent, concentrating on documentation for dynamic testing and is verifiable. It is independent of life cycle or method, but can be tailored down for small or low-risk developments. Additional standards would be required for the testing process and for testing methods, techniques and tools.

The examples and descriptions included make it a useful document.

IEEE 1012:1986 standard for software verification and validation plans

This Standard defines the tasks and documentation for a V&V Plan for both critical and non-critical software. Review and testing requirements for each phase of a model life-cycle are defined. The Standard is comprehensive, concise and clearly written. It has a particularly clear stucture of phase reviews and differentiates between critical and non-critical software. It would require modification to use non-IEEE terminology (it references other IEEE Standards).

Appendix 4
Methods, tools and techniques

STARTS guide, 2nd edition, 1987

This is a Guide to methods and software tools for software development work, produced to define 'best recommended practice' for software engineering. This edition is a total, more general purpose, revision of an earlier guide originally intended for real-time systems development. It uses a hierarchical life-cycle model which includes QA and Quality Management.

The Guide describes requirements for Quality Plans, including VV&T and Configuration Management. Project Management, Requirements Definition and Design are also included. In each case, detailed guidance is provided, followed by identification and assessments of relevant software tools, although this information is now somewhat out-of-date. Much of the information is applicable to IT as well as real-time systems.

Other guidance material

STARTS purchasers' handbook, second edition 1989

This Handbook outlines best practice in specifying and purchasing software-based systems. It contains useful advice and recommendations, aimed particularly at purchasing organisations. Topics include Procurement, Requirements Specification, Invitation to Tender, Product Acceptance as well as Maintenance practice. It also covers Project Management and Quality Assurance.

The Handbook adopts the same life-cycle model as the *STARTS Guide*. Safety-related systems and the use of metrics is included. Some parts (including the Quality Assurance chapter) could be used to verify a supplier's conformance.

IT STARTS developers guide, 1989

This Guide describes best current practice in the process of IT system development. It contains useful advice and recommendations aimed at many roles in IT development. It is based on the STARTS life-cycle model, but recognises alternative models such as Incremental Development and Prototyping.

There is extensive coverage of Quality Assurance and Project Management. The STARTS life cycle emphasises Analysis and Design and the testing aspects of program development. Alternative program development approaches and environments (3GLs, 4GLs, DBMS, KBS) are considered and compared. The Guide is generally not suitable for use as a verifiable Standard.

CCTA infrastructure library

The Central Computer and Telecommunications Agency (CCTA), part of H.M. Treasury, has developed a wide range of methods and associated guides. Initially intended for large government IT projects, these methods include SSADM for Systems Analysis and Design, PRINCE for Project Management and CRAMM for Risk Analysis. They have produced an IT Infrastructure Library, which is a series of guides and handbooks relating to the provision of IT services. They are intended to define good practice for IT service management. Documentation includes:

- *Managers' Set*
  (including Planning and Control, Quality Audit and Vendor Management)
- *Service Delivery Set*
  (including Service Level management)
- *Service Support Set*
  (including Problem and Change Management)
- *Computer Operations Set*
- *Networks*
- *Software Support*
  (including Applications Life-cycle and Testing Software for Operational Use)

The Infrastructure Library is intended to help an IT Services Group to comply with many of the ISO 9001 requirements, in particular:

- Process Control
- Handling, Storage, Packaging and Delivery
- Quality Records
- Internal Quality Audits
- Servicing

Many of the guides within the CCTA Infrastructure Library are published by John Wiley as part of their Information Systems (IS) Guides.

The TickIT guide – a guide to software QMS construction and certification using ISO 9001/EN29001/BS 5750 part 1 (1987)

This is a most important guidance document for software work produced in 1991 by the DTI TickIT project. It includes much explanatory information to help purchasers, suppliers and developers to understand and interpret the ISO 9001 Standard for software work (as well as inform its primary audience, Quality Systems Auditors).

The Guide includes a draft version (DIS 9000-2) of the ISO 9000-3 document *Guidelines for the application of ISO 9001 to the development, supply and maintenance of software.* It expresses Quality System requirements as framework, life-cycle and supporting activities (including Configuration Management). It includes specific guidance for suppliers, purchasers and auditors, with much detailed and practical information, such as Quality Assessment Schedules for performance of Quality System Audit.

In addition to the above, some professional and industry bodies have produced guides intended to help interpret and relate standards to the requirements of software engineering. These are useful in explaining general standards in software terms. Examples are:

EEA guide to the quality assurance of software (1978)

This Guide is intended for QA staff and non-specialist managers. It is structured as a table of events based on a simple life cycle, with activities indicated for the design team and quality representatives. It does not distinguish whether the quality representative is a project team member or from an external QA department. It is now somewhat dated, but is still a useful background document.

EEA guide to establishing a QA function for software (1981)

This Guide identifies Quality Control and Quality Assurance tasks relating to project and quality management, and examines the need for standards, tools and methods. However, it does not provide much detailed guidance for the software QA practitioner.

DEF STAN 00-16 guide to the achievement of quality in software (1980)

Although an MoD document, this is widely used in the software industry, providing useful advice and ideas for the practitioner. It covers the disciplines needed within a Quality System to provide software quality assurance. It pre-supposes the existence of a Quality System, and concentrates on aspects important to software quality.

The Guide is structured according to an overall life-cycle, identifying the controls needed at each phase including specification, planning and codes of practice with the appropriate QA considerations. Checklists supporting the principal activities are included.

Sources of standards

A comprehensive list of Software Engineering Public Domain Standards is available in the *STARTS Guide, 2nd Edition* (NCC), and from the UK Institution of Electrical Engineers (IEE). Most Standards can be obtained from:

>London Information
>Index House
>Ascot
>Berkshire
>SL5 7EU

Sources of Guidance material mentioned above:
>Institution of Electrical Engineers (IEE)
>P.O. Box 26
>Hitchin
>Herts SG5 1SA

STARTS Project:
>Sales Administration
>National Computing Centre
>Oxford Road
>Manchester M1 7ED

TickIT Project:
>TickIT Project Office
>68 Newman St
>London W1A 4SE

CCTA IT Infrastructure Library
>Information from:

>CCTA
>Gildengate House
>Upper Green Lane
>Norwich NR3 1DW

Appendix 4

Books can be ordered from:
>HMSO Books (P9D)
>FREEPOST
>Norwich NR3 1PD

CCTA IS Guides
>John Wiley & Sons Ltd
>Baffins Lane
>Chichester PO19 1UD

Appendix 5
Quality review and audit

Within software development the term 'Review' is often used widely; sometimes as a general term to include technical events such as Inspections, and for management events such as Project Review for evaluation of project progress.

Types of review

The following types of review are relevant to software development:

Technical review

This is an evaluation of a project deliverable (or equivalent) at the end of a work task. Examples are Inspections and Walkthroughs (i.e. peer reviews), or at a less formal level, 'desk-checks' by an author and an independent reviewer.

Management review

This is a management event to assess project progress and status against plans (e.g. End-of-phase Progress Review) and/or to review future plans to obtain approval. It involves the Project Manager, a more senior manager if approval is needed, usually a technical representative (e.g. team leader), and sometimes a customer or user representative.

Quality review

This is an evaluation of the compliance of the project to the Quality Plan, including standards, procedures and other requirements. It may include ensuring that the scheduled Technical Reviews have taken place, and provides input to the end-of-phase Management Review. Typically, it is performed by the Quality Manager (or QA person), with actions usually the responsibility of the Project Manager.

The term is also used to represent an evaluation of the effectiveness of an organisation's Quality System, based on the results of a set of quality audits of specific aspects of the Quality System operation (see below). Within a BS 5750 Quality System, it is the responsibility of the Quality Manager to perform such a Quality Review at least annually.

An individual project should define the required series of Technical, Management and Quality Reviews within the project plans.

Types of audit

Audit is a method of assessment; collecting and analysing information and then presenting recommendations which allow decisions to be made. It is a documented examination and analysis of objective evidence. In the context of a development project, Quality Audit is a method available to independent quality personnel (or someone acting in this role), typically to assess the extent of compliance of projects to Procedures, Standards, Quality Plans and other requirements of a Quality System.

Vertical and horizontal audit

A Vertical Audit examines some aspect of the Quality System on a specific project, for example project activities are traced sequentially for compliance with progress, project and any other plans. Non-compliances will usually result in corrective actions being agreed between the Project Manager and the QA person. Deficiencies in the Quality System (e.g. inadequate standards) can be forwarded for consideration at a Quality Review.

A Horizontal Audit looks at a single type of activity (e.g. design practice) across many projects. This allows the activity to be assessed more deeply than would be the case from a number of Vertical Audits. This type of audit is intended primarily to detect deficiencies in the Quality System.

Both types of audit should be planned as a programme such that an effective coverage of projects and the Quality System is achieved over a period of 6 or 12 months, and co-ordinated with the periodic Quality Review of the Quality System. Most of the matters arising at Review, and the evidence available, will have arisen from individual audits. (Vertical Audits may be more difficult to plan in advance because of the more uncertain nature of project work.)

Audit requirements of BS 5750/ISO 9001

Within a BS5750/ISO 9001-type Quality System, there is a requirement for two types of audit:

- internal
- external.

Internal Quality Systems Audit is performed on a first-party basis, i.e. the organisation, department or section covered by the Quality System audits itself (usually by means of project-independent quality personnel). External Audit is where a second-party (e.g. purchaser) or third-party (e.g. British Standards Institute) evaluates the Quality System from an external or completely independent viewpoint.

The value of an external Standard such as BS 5750/ISO 9001 is that it defines a set of requirements for a Quality System which are used as the basis of audit; is the Quality System defined and operated in a way which meets the requirements of ISO 9001? The content of the organisation's Quality System is defined in the Quality Manual and associated documentation, and becomes the second basis for Quality Systems Audit; does the operation of the Quality System comply with its own definition in the Quality Manual?

The role of the auditor

Within the audit process, the auditor has a key role. The DTI *TickIT Guide* for software Quality Systems explains the Auditor's role as being threefold:

- to confirm that the documented QMS has the capability to be used effectively in the management and products of the organisation;
- to confirm the use of the documented QMS in the management of current work by means of sample auditing;
- to confirm that the practices used within the QMS comply with the ISO 9001 methods and principles.

(The actual wording used here is a simplified version.)

An internal audit has similar objectives, but cannot formally address the third one stated above.

A Quality Systems Audit is organised in a similar way to other forms of audit:

- the objectives and/or terms of reference are defined;
- an auditor with sufficient management and financial independence is appointed;
- the auditor produces a plan of action (Audit Plan) which identifies the documentary evidence and "live" examination required;
- the auditor carries out this plan, although he may deviate from it (or examine in greater detail) where circumstances require.

Appendix 5

The audit will normally consist of two main stages: firstly, documentary evidence (e.g. project plans and records) is examined, then live examination of the project and organisational practice is performed (e.g. by interviewing project personnel, examining project practice).

All information obtained during audit is treated as confidential and only used for the purposes of the audit. This is particularly important where the auditor belongs to an external (third-party) organisation.

Appendix 6
References and further reading

Chapter 2

Principles of Software Engineering Management (1987) Tom Gilb, Addison-Wesley

STARTS Purchasers' Handbook (1989) National Computing Centre Ltd, Manchester

Chapter 3

BS 5750 Part 1/ISO 9001/EN 29001 Quality Systems; Specification for design/development, production, installation and servicing (1987), British Standards Institution, Milton Keynes MK14 6LE

TickIT Guide: Guide to Software Quality Management System Construction and Certification (1990), TickIT Project Office, 68 Newman St, London W1A 4SE

Chapter 4

Software Quality Assurance: Model Procedures (1990), IEE

Guidelines for the Documentation of Computer Software for Real-Time and Interactive Systems, 2nd Edition, 1990, IEE, P.O. Box 96, Stevenage, Herts SG1 2SD

Chapter 5

Software Inspection Handbook (1990), IEE

Chapter 6

Model Quality Management Manual (1989), Mitec Publishing, High St, Midsomer Norton, Bath BA3 2LE

Index

	Page
Acceptance	2, 18, 23, 42, 58, 62-64, 78, 96, 136-138, 147-149, 154, 164
Advantages	10, 11
Advisory	47, 48, 54
Amendment Methods	84, 86
Amendments	53, 76, 84-86, 143
ANSI/IEEE	68, 131, 161-163
ANSI/IEEE 730:1984	68, 161
ANSI/IEEE 828:1983	131, 161
ANSI/IEEE 829:1983	163
ANSI/IEEE 830:1983	162
ANSI/IEEE 983:1986	161
Appraisal	57, 119, 120
AQAP	67, 158, 159
AQAP 1	67, 158, 159
AQAP 13	67, 159
AQAP 14	159
AQAP 2	158
Assessment	3, 4, 8, 9, 18, 24, 32, 40, 67, 72, 80, 81, 86, 93, 94, 96, 100, 101, 105, 106, 107, 115, 116, 135, 148, 150, 158-160, 166, 170
Assessor	82, 86, 105-107
Audit	9, 31-32, 39, 41, 53, 55-57, 65-67, 72, 80-81, 87-88, 92, 105-106, 108, 127, 131-132, 147-149, 161, 165-166, 169-172
Audit Plan	171
Audit Requirements	170
Audit Trail	148
Auditor's Role	171
Author	55, 65, 69-71, 75-77, 128, 169

176   *Index*

Authorisation	50, 53, 55, 90-93, 96, 99, 123, 126-129, 133, 137, 151, 154
Authority	9, 28, 37, 61, 63, 64, 68, 85, 125, 129, 132
Awareness	100, 104, 121
Backup, Security and Archiving	57
Benefits	4, 5, 10, 11, 31, 63, 68, 69, 89, 99, 101, 103-107, 120, 121, 132, 135, 150
Bonding	128, 129
Brainstorming	115, 116
British Standards Institution (BSI)	2, 8, 67, 106, 158
BS 4778	14, 86
BS 5515	162, 163
BS 5750	6, 8-10, 18, 26, 27, 30-32, 40, 43-45, 50, 51, 54-56, 61-67, 80, 81, 83-86, 89-94, 99-107, 109-111, 124, 138, 147, 159, 165, 170, 171
BS 5750 Parts 0 to 3	26, 160
BS 5750 Part 1	27, 159, 166
BS 5882	160
BS 5887	163
Build Control	125
Building in Quality	3, 13
Cause and Effect	111, 113
CCTA Infrastructure Library	165
Certification	6, 8, 32, 67, 87, 101, 104-108, 159, 166
Certification Body	8, 67, 105, 106, 108
Change Assessment	94
Change Control	46, 52, 57, 58, 96, 126, 127, 129-131
Changes	4, 7, 9, 17, 20, 28, 29, 33, 37, 56, 76, 77, 79, 82, 84, 87, 90, 96, 100, 102-105, 107, 109, 115, 123, 124, 128, 129, 132, 133, 137, 139, 147, 161
Changing methods and practices	103
Characteristics	14, 19-24, 63
Checklist	22, 77, 78, 87, 105-107, 150, 152-154
Checklist questions	22, 78, 152
Code of Practice	46, 48, 54, 162, 163
Commercial Advantage	6, 45
Company Description	84
Company Organisation	86
Compliance to Requirements	11
Confidence	1-4, 7, 8, 10, 31, 66, 82, 86, 129
Confidentiality	38, 45, 82, 84
Configuration Audit	127
Configuration Identification	128
Configuration Items	93, 124, 125, 128, 130

Configuration Librarian	125, 128, 129
Configuration Management	42, 57, 93, 96, 123-129, 131-133, 142, 157, 159-162, 164, 166
Configuration Management Plans	131
Configuration Management System	124-128, 132
Configuration Management Tools	126, 131
Conformance	11, 12, 17, 18, 32, 109, 150, 164
Continuous Improvement	110, 111
Contract Review	15, 32, 42, 55, 102, 138
Contractors	8, 27, 38, 159
Contractual Documents	91
Corrective Action	31, 32, 41, 55, 57, 61, 64, 66, 80, 94, 97, 105, 107, 109, 120, 147, 148
Cost of Failure	18
Costs	4, 39, 96, 103, 104, 108, 118-121
Criteria	21, 23, 24, 43, 54, 62, 63, 70, 72, 75, 78, 79, 95, 138, 149, 151
Critical Design Review	68
Culture	9, 112
Customer/User	71, 96
Customers' Needs	21
DEF STAN 00-16	166
DEF STAN 05-21	158
Defect Control	94
Defect Recording	18
Defects	13, 36, 39, 41, 42, 63-65, 67, 69-71, 73-76, 79, 80, 93, 94, 105, 117, 121
Delegation of Authority	28
Delivery	16, 24, 26, 29, 35, 36, 42, 56, 58, 78, 90, 93, 117, 128, 129, 133, 138, 140, 158, 165
Department of Trade and Industry; see DTI	
Design and Development	6, 26, 33, 61, 62, 65, 85, 159
Design and Implementation	42
Design Control	33, 56, 124, 138
Design Reviews	18, 63-65, 77
Detection of Defects	13, 64, 69, 75
Developer	1, 2, 6, 11-13, 15, 18, 21, 22, 34, 43, 66, 97, 115, 116, 125, 135, 136
Development Life-Cycle	13, 36, 58, 61, 64, 80, 128, 162
Development Methods	1, 137, 142
Development Planning	33, 42
Development Process	5, 13-15, 26, 33, 35-37, 41, 62, 64, 65
DIS 9000-2	40, 166
Distribution	31, 57, 84, 86, 124
Distribution and Amendment Methods	84, 86

Index

Document Control	24, 37, 41, 42, 56, 86, 110, 124, 130
Document List (see also Documentation Index)	92
Document Review and Control	92
Documentation	8, 25, 31, 33, 36, 37, 42, 45, 47-54, 56-61, 66, 67, 69, 72, 74, 81-84, 86, 87, 88, 92, 93, 95, 96, 100, 106, 107, 115, 123-125, 129, 130, 131-133, 149, 150, 157, 162, 163, 165, 171
Documentation Format	52
Documentation Index (see also Document List)	51, 87
Documentation Librarian	51
Documentation Standards	49, 57, 60, 82, 149, 150, 163
Documentation Structure	81, 87
Documentation System	129, 163
Documenting the Quality System	81
DTI	5, 40, 99, 106, 159, 166, 171
Education and Training	104
EEA Guide to Software Configuration Management	162
EN 29000 series (see also BS 5750)	8, 26, 27
Enhancement Life-Cycle	142
Error List	78
Escalation of Problems	3
Evaluation	17, 57, 64-69, 77-79, 92, 150, 158, 159, 161, 169, 170
Evolution	93, 126, 142
Excellence (Quality as)	11
Experience	2, 7, 13, 31, 39, 45, 63, 69, 78, 81, 101, 106, 108, 141, 148, 150
External Assessment	8, 32
Factors	1, 2, 11, 21, 22, 25, 39, 82, 101, 117, 123
Fagan Inspection	68, 69, 76
Failure Costs	119
Failure Rate	17, 113, 114
Faults and Problems	1
Files	6, 16, 35, 95, 125, 128, 132, 148
Fitness for Purpose	5, 11, 13, 15
Force-Field Analysis	117
Fourth Generation Languages (4GLs)	137, 157
Guidance	40, 43, 50, 54, 58-59, 86-88, 102, 150, 157-159, 162, 164, 166, 167
Handling of Defects	63
Handling, Storage, Packaging and Delivery	35, 56, 165
Horizontal Audit	170
How-How Technique	117

Identification	32, 36, 50-52, 56, 57, 61, 63, 64, 79, 84, 86, 88, 90-93, 95, 121, 123-125, 127, 128, 131, 132, 164
Identification Standard	50
Identifier	38, 50-52, 128, 132, 149, 154
IEEE	68, 131, 161-163
IEEE 1012:1986	163
Importance of Quality	5
Importance of Software	5
Improvement	6, 9, 10, 13, 18, 23, 32, 33, 39, 46, 57, 76, 79, 80, 85, 99-102, 105, 107, 108-112, 115, 117, 120, 121, 159
Improvement Review	80
Included Software Product	43
Incremental Approach (to Life-Cycle)	140
Independent QA	3, 87, 91, 92
Indicators of Quality	16
Inspection	4, 9, 10, 23, 24, 26, 30, 32, 34, 35, 37, 39, 56-58, 61-65, 68-80, 92, 102, 104, 111, 117, 119, 124, 130, 138, 147-151, 153, 169
Inspection and Review Invitation	149, 151
Inspection and Review Report	153
Inspection and Test	26, 32, 34, 35, 37, 61, 62, 102, 124
Inspection Criteria	75, 79, 149
Inspection Records	80, 130
Internal Quality Audits	32, 39, 55, 165
International Standards	8, 26, 59
International Standards Organisation (ISO)	59
Introducing a Quality System	7, 10, 99-101, 105
ISO 9000 series: see BS 5750	
ISO 9000-32	8, 40, 41, 86, 124, 128, 130, 138, 160, 166
ISO 9001: see BS 5750 Part 1	
IT Systems	5, 8, 99, 137, 142
JSP 188	162
Levels of Control	65
Life-Cycle Approach	13, 141, 142
Life-Cycle Documentation	157
Life-Cycle Methods	13, 43
Life-Cycle Model	16, 33, 61, 87, 90, 103, 129, 135-138, 142, 161, 163, 164
List of Contents	84, 85
Maintenance	6, 19, 20, 33, 42, 56, 57, 58, 62, 72, 80, 85, 91, 95-97, 100, 107, 127, 130, 135-137, 143, 148, 160, 162, 164, 166
Management Responsibilities	9, 28, 32, 41, 82

180   *Index*

Management Review	31, 67, 169
Mandatory Plan	6
Manufactured Product Quality	17
Manufacturing	4, 6-8, 14-16, 26, 35, 38
Materials	6, 11, 15, 16, 38
Maturity	8, 10
Measurable	13
Measurements	6, 18, 22, 23, 35, 42, 135, 160
Measuring and Test Equipment	35, 56
Measuring Software Quality	16
Media	26, 36, 93
Methods	1, 3, 6-8, 13, 16, 25, 27, 33, 34, 42, 43, 47, 54, 58, 79, 84-86, 90, 93, 94, 96, 103, 108, 110, 112, 125, 129, 135-138, 141, 142, 157, 159, 162-166, 171
MIL-STD-1535A	160
Milestones	3
Ministry of Defence (MoD)	8, 67, 158, 159, 166
Moderator	71, 72, 74-77, 79, 151, 153
NATO	8, 67, 158, 159
Non-conforming Product	32, 35, 37, 56, 63, 124, 138
Operating Instructions	82
Operational	1, 5, 6, 9, 11, 12, 14, 16, 22, 26, 28, 31, 42, 52, 63, 66, 80, 82, 101, 104, 105, 116, 127, 163, 165
Organisational Objectives	6
Peer Review	68, 69, 92
Peer Reviewer	69, 71, 73
Personnel Roles	71
Phase Outputs	138
Pre-emptive	6, 109
Presenter	71
Prevention	79, 119, 120
Prevention Techniques	77
Problem Handling	97
Problem Reporting	94, 127
Problem Reports	116, 148, 150
Problem Solving	120
Problems	1, 3, 4, 8, 9, 13, 17, 25, 32-34, 41, 46, 64, 69, 70, 73, 74, 78-80, 94, 100, 103-105, 108, 110, 112, 114, 115, 117, 121, 123, 127, 133, 138, 141, 147, 148
Procedure Content	53

Procedures	4, 8, 9, 12, 22, 29-39, 43-62, 66, 67, 72, 77, 80-83, 85, 87, 88, 90-92, 94, 96, 100-102, 104, 107-109, 111, 115, 125, 129-131, 135, 138, 142, 143, 147, 148, 150, 154, 162, 169, 170
Procedures Index	51, 57
Procedures Manuals	8, 82, 91
Process(es)	5-10, 13-16, 18, 20, 22, 24, 26, 27, 29-38, 41, 45, 46, 48, 50, 51, 54-56, 61, 62, 64-68, 71-73, 79, 80, 87, 94, 96, 99, 100, 105, 106, 108-117, 127, 137, 138, 160, 163-165, 171
Process Control	33, 56, 138, 165
Procurement (see also Purchasing)	57, 159, 164
Product Characteristics	19
Product Control	93, 123, 125
Product Development	15, 16, 19, 64
Product Identification	36, 56, 124
Product Quality	1, 3, 12, 14, 17-19, 21, 24, 29, 31, 40, 61, 110, 111, 135, 147, 148
Product Requirements	7, 12, 18-20, 23
Product Specification	16, 18, 78
Production	6-8, 26, 33, 92, 100, 119, 131, 159, 161
Productivity	4, 69, 80, 120, 121, 126
Progress Monitoring and Reporting	96
Project Control Plan	78, 92, 96
Project Description	90
Project Files	148
Project Initiation	15, 32, 58, 99
Project Librarian	125
Project Library	93, 125, 128, 131, 152
Project Manager	3, 8, 9, 46, 50, 70, 71, 74, 77, 87, 88, 90, 97, 100, 102, 103, 128, 129, 148, 154, 169, 170
Project Manager's Responsibilities	8
Project Phases	52
Project Plans	1-3, 33, 91, 104, 111, 130, 137, 170, 172
Project Quality Plan	8, 9, 39, 42, 46, 53, 63, 71, 72, 83, 88-90, 97, 137, 142, 143, 148, 161
Project Requirements	15, 125, 128, 138
Project Reviews	3, 9, 41, 67, 96, 97
Project Technical Plan	94
Project Test Plan	62, 64, 92, 95
Proposals	2, 87
Purchaser	1-10, 11-13, 20, 25, 27, 38, 39, 41-44, 56, 58, 62, 66, 82, 90, 91, 96, 97, 111, 119, 130, 135, 136, 140, 147, 159, 171
Purchaser and Supplier	1, 4, 42, 140
Purchaser Involvement	5, 97

Index

Purchaser Participation	3
Purchaser Requirements	2, 10, 13, 42
Purchaser's Responsibility	12
Purchaser-Supplied Product	38, 56
Purchasers' Handbook (STARTS)	161, 164
Purchasing (see also Procurement)	38, 43, 57, 67, 96, 164
QA Function	3, 28, 166
Qualifications	39, 40, 63, 91
Quality Assurance	1, 4, 7, 10, 28, 68, 71, 72, 86-88, 92, 94, 142, 148, 160, 161, 164, 166, 167
Quality Assurance Department (see also QA Function)	71
Quality Audits	32, 39, 55, 165, 170
Quality Characteristics	23, 24
Quality Control	1, 3-5, 7, 9, 10, 45, 58, 61, 62, 68, 80, 86-88, 92, 94, 108, 109, 111, 117, 119, 123, 142, 158, 159, 166
Quality Costs	118, 120
Quality Costs Initiative	120
Quality Engineer	37, 128
Quality File	76, 78, 150
Quality Forms	149, 150
Quality Improvement	6, 9, 10, 23, 99, 101, 108-112, 121
Quality in Software	166
Quality Information	121
Quality Log	148
Quality Management	1, 2, 4-7, 10, 16, 18, 26, 28, 55, 80, 87, 88, 91 94, 96, 99, 108-110, 129, 157, 158, 160, 164, 166
Quality Manager	3, 9, 28, 29, 31, 32, 37, 46, 50, 51, 66, 84, 86, 91, 97, 100, 102, 105, 129, 169, 170
Quality Manual	8, 28, 31, 45, 57, 66, 67, 81-83, 85-88, 91, 102, 103, 171
Quality Manual Content	87
Quality Measurement	18
Quality Objectives	28
Quality of Product	13, 14, 65, 110
Quality of Software	6, 7
Quality Plan(s)	3, 4 ,6-9, 13, 30, 31, 39, 41, 42, 45, 46, 48, 53, 57, 61-63, 71, 72, 75, 81, 83, 87-92, 94, 95-97, 130, 137, 142, 143, 148, 161, 164, 169, 170
Quality Plan Headings	89
Quality Plan Management	90, 91
Quality Planning	42, 142, 157, 161
Quality Policy	28, 29, 31, 57, 82, 84, 85, 102, 103

Quality Programme	82, 108, 110, 111, 120
Quality Records	32, 39, 42, 56, 63, 67, 78, 88, 95, 111, 112, 147, 148, 153, 165
Quality Requirements	2, 14, 19, 24, 88, 121, 135
Quality Responsibility	112
Quality Review	169, 170
Quality Staff	9
Quality System	2, 4-10, 13, 24-33, 37, 39-46, 48, 50-52, 54-57, 59, 61, 63, 65-67, 69, 72, 80-91, 99-112, 120, 121, 129, 130, 133, 138, 142, 143, 147, 148, 149, 155, 157-161, 166, 167, 170, 171
Quality System Assessment	67
Quality System Audit	9, 31, 41, 66, 67, 105, 106, 108, 147-149, 166, 171
Quality-related Practices	4, 5, 8-10
Reactive	6, 109
Record of Amendments	84, 85
Registration (see also Certification)	8, 67, 84, 128, 129
Releases	37, 84, 125, 126, 128, 131
Reliability	1, 12, 17-19, 22
Requirements	1, 2, 7-10, 11-15, 17-24, 27, 28, 32-43, 45, 46, 49-56, 58-59, 61-64, 66-69, 72-75, 78, 79, 86, 88-92, 95, 96, 101, 102, 105, 109, 110, 121, 123-125, 128, 130, 131, 135-139, 141, 142, 148, 149, 157, 158-166, 169-171
Resources	6, 15, 19, 32, 61, 64, 68, 96, 101, 103, 104, 119, 135, 136
Responsibilities	2, 8, 9, 28, 29, 31-33, 45, 64, 82, 86, 88, 90, 91, 94-97, 105, 112, 131, 135
Review(s)	1, 3-5, 7-9, 15, 18, 19, 22-24, 30-33, 39, 41-43, 46, 51, 53, 55-58, 61, 63-65, 67-69, 72, 74, 76-81, 87, 88, 90-92, 94, 96, 97, 100, 102, 103, 107, 109, 114, 115, 117, 120, 130, 138, 141, 147-154, 159-161, 163, 169, 170
Review Checklist	152
Reviews and Audits	64, 161
Rules, Practices and Conventions	43
Savings	6, 69, 80
Second Party	8
Security	22, 57, 93, 132
Servicing	36, 56, 138, 159, 165
Skills and Experience	7
Software Configuration Management	123, 161, 162
Software Control	93

184 Index

Software Engineering	13, 157, 158, 164, 166, 167
Software Life-Cycle	41, 137
Software Metrics	18
Software Product Usage	18
Software Quality	1, 6, 11, 16-18, 22, 68, 157, 159, 161, 166, 167, 171
Software Quality Assurance	68, 161, 166
Software Release	123
Software Requirements	15, 68, 162, 163
Software Verification and Validation	163
Specification	6, 8, 16, 18, 22, 26, 35, 36, 42, 58, 66, 68, 77-80, 128, 136, 140, 150, 159, 160, 162-164, 167
Stage(s)	3, 6, 10, 13, 15, 16, 33, 34, 36, 38, 46, 53, 57, 58, 61, 62, 66, 68, 69, 72, 75, 80, 85, 90, 94, 96, 97, 100-107, 113, 116, 135, 137, 150, 158, 162, 172
Stages of Inspection	34, 72
Standard(s)	1, 2, 4, 8-10, 11, 12, 14, 15, 18, 25-35, 37-40, 43-63, 67, 68, 71-73, 75, 78, 80-83, 85, 87-92, 94, 104, 106, 107, 109, 110, 117, 124, 129, 131, 135, 137, 138, 142, 143, 147, 149-151, 157-163, 165-167, 169-171
Standards, Procedures and Working Practices	92
STARTS	3, 6, 13, 14, 72, 74, 161, 164, 167
Statement of Quality Policy	84, 85
Statistical Measures	18
Statistical Techniques	39, 56
Status Accounting and Reporting	126
Steering Committee	100, 120
Storage and Custody	93
Structure and Content of Procedures	48
Sub-contractors	27, 38
Supplier	1-10, 11-13, 27, 29, 31, 33, 36, 38, 39, 41, 42, 57, 81, 82, 94-96, 103, 111, 135, 136, 140, 147, 159-161, 164
Supplier Control	94, 103, 161
Supplier QA	3
Supplier Quality System	2, 4, 8
Supplier Responsibilities	96
Supplier Visibility	5
Supplier's Approach to Development	2
Supplier/Developer Responsibility	12
Surveillance	3, 108
System and Acceptance Testing	18
System Build	124
System Releases	128

Team Leader	63, 68, 71, 77, 97, 128, 169
Technical Publications	162
Technical Review(s)	64, 65, 67, 68, 159, 169
Techniques and Methods	16, 159
Test Management	95
Test Plan	18, 62, 64, 65, 77, 78, 88, 92, 95
Test Records	9, 35, 62, 63, 96, 110
Test Requirements	12, 23, 95
Test Specification	68
Testing	7, 9, 13, 16-18, 22, 24, 25, 31, 34, 42, 47, 56, 58, 61-65, 69, 70, 75, 80, 83, 90, 92, 111, 116, 117, 119, 124, 136-140, 163-165
Testing and Validation	42
Third Party	8, 72, 159, 171
TickIT	40, 43, 106, 159, 166, 167, 171
TickIT Guide	40, 43, 166, 171
Time-Dependent Measures	18
Tools and Techniques	43, 90, 94, 157, 164
Total Quality Management	5, 6, 10, 99, 108-110
Traceability	18, 36, 56, 124, 128, 131
Trade-off	15
Training	22, 39, 40, 43, 56-58, 69, 100, 102, 104, 107, 121, 148
Trend Analysis	18, 39
User Representative	72, 77, 78, 129, 169
User Requirements	15, 58, 141
Verification	18, 29, 31, 33, 34, 54, 56, 58, 61-65, 68, 69, 94, 124, 130, 138, 142, 147, 157, 163
Verification Activities	63, 64
Verification Authority	63, 64
Verification, Validation and Test	64, 157
Version Control	57, 125
Vertical Audit	170
Viewpoint(s)	21, 34, 71, 74, 110, 111, 136, 171
Visibility	4, 5
Walkthroughs	58, 64, 65, 92, 169
Waterfall Model	139
Why-Why Technique	116, 117
Work Instruction	46, 47
Work Tasks	3, 9, 68, 82, 104, 148
Working Practices	9, 25, 27, 30, 45, 51, 82, 92, 104
Workmanship	6, 113